# WHERE THE RAIN
# CHILDREN SLEEP

*"Alone in the natural world, time is less dense, less filled with information; space is close; smell and hearing and touch reassert themselves. The wild is keenly sensual. In a true wilderness we are like that much of the time, even in broad daylight. Alert, careful, literally 'full of care'. Not because of principles, but because of something very old."*

—Jack Turner, writer and mountain guide

*"I am ashamed before the heavens;*
*I am ashamed before the dawn;*
*I am ashamed before the evening twilight;*
*I am ashamed before the blue sky;*
*I am ashamed before the sun.*
*I am ashamed before that standing within me*
*which speaks with me.*
*Some of these things are always looking at me.*
*I am never out of sight.*
*Therefore I must tell the truth.*
*I hold my word tight to my breast."*

—Old Torlino, Diné elder

# WHERE THE RAIN CHILDREN SLEEP

≈≈≈

## A SACRED GEOGRAPHY OF THE COLORADO PLATEAU

*Michael Engelhard*

### THE LYONS PRESS

Guilford, Connecticut
An imprint of The Globe Pequot Press

The Lyons Press is an imprint of The Globe Pequot Press

10  9  8  7  6  5  4  3  2  1

Printed in the United States of America

ISBN 1-59228-261-X

Library of Congress Cataloging-in-Publication Data is available
on file.

# CONTENTS

# PREFACE

*"The traveler is unworthy of his privilege, and forgetful of his duty, if he extracts not from the scenes some moral lessons or religious truth."*

—Thomas Cole, painter

OCCASIONALLY, ACQUAINTANCES ASK ABOUT MY RELIGIOUS affiliation. "I am a Blue Domer," I tell them. Some simply shrug, dismissing this as clever wordplay or a fondness for metaphor. But it is true. The prodigious desert sky forms the vault under which I worship. Unexpectedly, birdsong rises from the land. It blends with the jubilations of crickets, the soaring and dipping phrases of coyotes, the rustling of cottonwoods—in a polyphony that praises creation. On a blistering summer day, the shade of an overhang promises salvation. Eternity stares from the beady eyes of a lizard; the incense of cedar and sage soothes my lungs. Alcoves hide plunge pools of transforming power, rimmed by smooth rock like Romanic baptismal fonts. With the luminescence of stained-glass windows, evening inflames cliff bands and willow thickets. It alights on water gathered in potholes. The cathedrals and temples of sandstone and shale that are my destinations, were already crumbling when believers still slept as unformed clay.

I have listened carefully to the old songs and stories. I know this land is hallowed. Its rivers run red with the menstrual blood of

First Woman. Its convolutions mark the proceedings of gods. Here, invisible strands radiating from places of power catch the dreaming of different races. Sacrilege and sacrifice follow each other. Each breath is prayer; every step leads to the center. This world is held fast by sacred mountains in all directions. Buttes and mesas, ridgelines and headlands steeped in myths form compass points that help me align my life.

Far from being religious in any orthodox sense, I have found the essence of wild places to elude purely secular language. At times, words fail entirely, and we can partake of this essence only through our bodies. In a similar manner, it seems to defy thinking, which is strictly rational, linear. I have finally come to realize that—across cultures and time—the vocabulary for the sublime in Nature may vary, while its impact on us does not.

In one of his novels Jonathan Carroll muses, "if you are very lucky, you're allowed to be in certain places during just the right season of your life." That is exactly how I feel about my time on the Colorado Plateau. And the right season for me by now has lasted close to twenty years.

My first encounter with the Redrock Desert still stands out in my mind. I toured the Grand Circle, largely sticking to three-starred attractions that could be reached by paved highways: Arches. Capitol Reef. Mesa Verde. Grand Canyon. Zion. I slept mostly in campgrounds rather than the backcountry. But at least I managed to stay away from motels. I got stoned for the first—and last—time, at Natural Bridges. I watched bug-eyed, as rock spans turned rubbery and the canyon bottom convulsed. In Bryce Canyon I raced a guy, speed-hiking the Below-the-Rim Trail. I was snowed in at the South Rim of the Grand Canyon, huddled in a car with a Japanese couple who shared their sushi with me. Less than a day later, I marveled at butterflies and golden leaves dancing at the bottom of the great chasm. Descending for the first time from the rim to Phantom Ranch felt like returning to a loved childhood place: a homecoming mixed with a sense of exploration. On Second Mesa, a Hopi family took me in for a memorable week. They offered a chance to learn about kachina carving, and about exquisite polychrome pottery, fired in kilns fed with dried sheep dung. The lessons that really stuck, however, were those of hospitality and strength drawn from the land. Before I realized, this high desert had hooked its sweet spines under my skin. But life had me sidetracking for a little longer.

Seven years later, after a stint in Europe as a potter and an aborted career as a cop, I was driving with my parents through Escalante when it had not yet become a national monument and tourist magnet. I was glued to the car window, craning my neck to follow the sweeping contours of slickrock that enfolded the highway. "I will have to come back," I thought, "to live in this region."

And I did. Moab became a base camp of sorts. Passion quickly turned into obsession. I felt fortunate, as this magnificent and reclusive landscape became not only my domicile but also my workplace. It would never cease to intrigue me with intricacies and moods that remain hidden to the casual visitor. During summers, I spent more days on the river than in town. My working outfit consisted of sandals and shorts. People's faces often lit up with envy when I asked them to step into my "office."

Sooner or later, my explorations had to lead to "Lake" Powell, and when they did, I was appalled. Approaching its stagnant waters for the first time in lower Swett Creek, I was shaken by the sight of three cormorants perched on the bones of a half-submerged cottonwood tree. Dulled by a leaden sky, they looked black and forlorn, like lost shadows, or ghosts. I could not believe my eyes. One-hundred-and-some tributary canyons had been inundated—so that strawberries and lettuce could be grown in the desert and city lights compete with the stars?

In a fit, I hiked the same number of canyons within one year, quitting my job in the process. It was the only way to comprehend the magnitude of loss, which would otherwise have remained an abstraction. I soon realized that the damming of the Colorado River in Glen Canyon had only been the most traumatizing act in the struggle for the soul of the Southwest. In less visible yet more insidious ways, cattle, developers, mismanagement, mining, industrial tourism, and a host of other assailants are still devouring this seemingly incorruptible desert, while we stand by and watch.

The essays in this volume spring from a growing concern that the song of the land, the stories and voices of these places, and their nonhuman and indigenous inhabitants might not be heard, against the din of bulldozers, powerboats, turbines, and four-wheelers. The following pages are but a small gesture of gratefulness, of remembering what has been given to me. I wish all readers were equally lucky, encountering the topography of their desire at the appropriate time in life.

# ACKNOWLEDGMENTS

P UTTING TOGETHER A BOOK IS A LOT LIKE FORMING A HUMAN pyramid—a collective balancing act. Without many strong, supportive shoulders, the entire structure would topple.

First and foremost, I would like to thank the indigenous people of the Colorado Plateau, whose stories continue to enrich my writing and life. Their hospitality has saved me numerous times from being stranded, while hitchhiking in the back-of-beyond. Joe Devin of Tsaile deserves special mention here, for clarifying Diné concepts of history and mythology for me.

In Moab, Dirk and Devin Vaughan provided transportation when it was badly needed and were forgiving when I damaged their craft. José Knighton did not mind me browsing his shelves, always eager to share insights into the book business. While I was looking for a publisher, Sara Melnicoff jokingly suggested I turn this into a love story, to increase its appeal. I did, and think it's a better book for it. The all-female star team of the Grand County, Utah, public library kept the stream of interlibrary loans flowing, and me from losing my mind over computer malfunctions.

Kudos also go to my hiking companion Morris Wolf in Hanksville, for putting up with my moods and extremist opinions, as well as with frequent note-taking breaks on the trail.

Jamie Bellermann, Stephen Bodio, Janice Bowers, and Dave Petersen read and commented upon various drafts of the manuscript, encouraging me to persist. I am likewise greatly indebted to

Clarke Abbey, for reading my homage to, and critique of Ed, in "Down the River with Ed and the Major." Carol Haralson of the Museum of Northern Arizona and Diane Kelly of the Southern Utah Wilderness Alliance, as well as Scott Slovic of the University of Nevada's Department of English, earned my gratitude by providing a forum for my writing. Carol also first suggested an essay about Sunset Crater.

Jayne Belnap of the U.S. Geological Survey's Biological Resources Division enlightened me about biological soil crusts (by way of Sandra Scott); Mark Miller of the same institution checked my facts in regard to the salinity of desert soils and helped with plant zonation. Ekkehart Malotki of Northern Arizona University assisted with sources and information about the Hopi Salt Pilgrimage route. At the Cline Library's Special Collections, Richard Quartaroli xeroxed sheaves of pages from dusty tomes and kindly forwarded them to me.

Tony and Nick Lyons defied market trends, taking on yet another collection of nature essays. Final thanks go to my editor, Tom McCarthy, who helped saving the vision into print.

Their contributions are greatly appreciated. Any shortcomings, biases, or errors should only be credited to myself.

Versions of some of these essays previously appeared in *Northern Lights Magazine* ("Splendid Desolation"), *Plateau Journal* ("Where the Rain Children Sleep"; "In Limbo," as "Hidden Passages"), *Redrock Wilderness* ("Beelzebub's Weekend Retreat"), *ISLE* ("Wind," as "Breath of Life, Breath of Death"; "A Salt Pilgrimage"), and *Hidden Passage* ("Fish in a Dry Place").

# WHERE THE RAIN
# CHILDREN SLEEP

# 1

# KACHINAS AND CINDER CONES

*"Social scientists are often loath to seek the significant impulses in human affairs among those events in nature that are commonly referred to as acts of God."*

—Don E. Dumond, archaeologist

T HROUGHOUT THE MOON OF FIRST FROST, ANIMALS HAD behaved strangely. The dogs kept up a whine, slinking around nervously, tails tucked between legs. Turkeys penned near the entrances of sod-covered houses never ceased gobbling or ruffling their feathers. Babies cried more than normal. Most of the deer upon which people depended had mysteriously disappeared. Even the small ground-burrowers were gone.

The evergreen forest lay sullen and silent.

A few days ago, Earth Mother had begun to tremble. Spasms rippled through her, as if she were about to give birth to some unspeakable monstrosity. Foul-smelling vapors started to pour from fissures in the ground, overlaid by whistling and hissing. Clay pots swollen with corn ears had shattered, spilling their gold-red-and-blue content. Ceilings and floors danced, until dirt sifted from cracks in the roofs. The tremor gripping their world took root deep inside people's bones. Priests consulted the oracles, to see which age-old taboos had been broken to disturb the gods. With shaking hands, they dropped cornmeal and feathered sticks into earth's angry ruptures, imploring the Powerful Ones to show mercy. People averted their eyes from the dark wall of the mountains. They uttered prayers under their breath.

They decided to leave. As if in a fever, every able-bodied person packed baskets of corn. Gourds filled with water. Fire drills, adzes, and arrowheads. Yucca mats, spare sandals. Bundles of dried deer meat. Rabbit fur blankets, to muffle the bite of the high desert night. They even took the heavy rock slabs used to grind corn and wild seeds. Some dismantled precious beams from their pit houses, so that new dwellings could be built elsewhere. Refugees trickled from homes that dotted the valley like wildflowers in spring. Bent under their loads, admonished by ominous rumblings, they hurried north. They left the bones of their ancestors with the snow-clad mountain range.

Later, safe in the low country, they rested, drowning in memories of familiar places that now lay forsaken. Turning to face the old homesteads, they beheld a spectacle many of them would still recall as old women and men.

The earth seemed to have split like a ripe melon. Thunderclaps racked the sky, while a red mouth belched columns of greasy, black smoke. Glowing tongues licked the bellies of clouds; lightning illuminated their insides. And a roaring reminiscent of waterfalls deafened the ears.

According to myth, a previous world had been destroyed by flood. Only a few righteous ones escaped the reckoning that time. Was this then the demise of the present—the fourth—world, as foretold in the ancient prophecies? Could this be the rain of fire that would end all, forever?

Night fell too early. Torrents of wind raged, bearing the sting of burned juniper. Raining ash. Smudging the skin of spectators. Graying hair prematurely. As the distant fire continued to sputter, embers and sparks spewed into every direction. Dull light coated faces, like blood.

In 1066 A.D., the year after the great conflagration, in a world beyond their world—and imagination—an army of Norman invaders vanquished an Anglo-Saxon host at the battle of Hastings.

Sunset Crater squats at the fringe of the relatively young San Francisco Volcanic Field, demarcating the fiery southern edge of the Colorado Plateau. Crowded by several hundred lesser cinder cones, it is the last one to have been active. Clusters of mounds dot the expanse sweeping from the San Francisco Peaks to the groove of the Little Colorado River in the east. Hopi speakers refer to these knobby protrusions as the Testicle Hills. They are telltale remains of several million years of volcanic activity in a region geologists still consider volatile. Though presently dormant, seismometers positioned throughout the field carefully monitor its activity. Volcanologists expect a new cone to sprout from these plains anytime in the future.

The dominating summits hover 12,500 feet above foothills that waver in sun glare. They owe their rugged symmetry to a final outburst of basaltic lavas, less than half a million years ago. Over time, erosion wore down the original pyramid that peaked over 16,000 feet into the desert blue.

I survey the scene of the Sinagua culture's exodus of more than nine hundred years ago, propped against a pile of boulders on top of O'Leary Peak, north of the gaping cone. This is the only place high and close enough to peer into Sunset Crater.

Wind soughs in stately ponderosa pines, muted like distant surf. The land below lies peaceful again, though scarred, blistered, and scabbed over. Barely covered by a skimpy skirt of evergreens, it still appears vulnerable. From up high the crater is revealed as less than perfect. Where lava broke through its walls, the rim has sagged, and its melted extrusions sealed off Bonito Park, seeking the lowest level to come to rest. I can easily spot cones that are more symmetrical from my vantage point. Shit Pot is one of them. Named with a cowboy sense of humor, the park service prudishly refers to it as S. P. Crater. Sunset Crater, however, stands out in its ruddy countenance. To the north, Highway 89 bisects the chain of the Testicle Hills, as well as the lion-skin plains and pastel warps of the Painted Desert. Hazy distance dulls the farthest outlines of this tableau.

As the sun lowers itself toward the brink of the earth, the wind retires for the night. The contrast between the volcano's tinted crown and dark base briefly intensifies. But inevitably, shadows pool inside the crater and the day is extinguished.

The story lines of indigenous people, of cultural anthropologists, explorers, volcanologists, paleobotanists, archaeologists, and even filmmakers, converge upon Sunset Crater like radial strands in a spider's web. Major John Wesley Powell christened this naked, but pleasing landmark, which forms the centerpiece of Sunset Crater Volcano National Monument, in 1879. Oxidized cinders surrounding the rim lend a russet and yellowish cast to its crest. It reminded the Major of afterglow in a western sky. The Hopi already knew this stump of a mountain as Palatsmo, or Red Hill.

Abnormal growth rings in trees that survived the initial firestorm have been used to establish dates for the dramatic events. According to this dendrochronology, sometime during the late fall or winter of 1064–65 A.D., lava exploded from a six-mile-long fissure. Gas trapped in the fiery flow burst as it rose to the surface. It ripped open the vent. Small fragments were flung into the atmosphere, cooled rapidly, and rained back down. They assembled a cone—one thousand feet high. Larger lumps cooled more slowly and were rounded into missiles, which pitted the landscape. Erratic winds spread the accompanying ash, smothering more than eight hundred square miles. As far away as sixty-three miles from the white-hot center of mayhem, fine dust fell onto the Hopi mesas. The first, highly explosive phase is thought to have lasted almost a quarter century, and only as late as 1250 A.D. did the tortured earth finally settle down.

Throughout the world, people have revered mountains for their spiritual power, considering them the domain of gods or supernatural beings. The San Francisco Peaks are no exception. To this day, the Hopi of north-central Arizona collect ingredients for their ceremonies, such as fir boughs, water, and soil there. They go on annual pilgrimages for this purpose. Individual names, assigned to most prominent points, help them to memorize the route. High above the plains, archaeologists unearthed ruins of a pit house and kiva, flanked by rock piles resembling Hopi shrines. These have been interpreted as remains of a ceremonial center of the Sinagua, pre-Columbian ancestors of the Hopi. Contemporary with the Anasazi farther north, they were named after the Spanish term for their home range, Sierra sin agua: Mountains-without-Water.

The Hopi have long regarded the ice-bound summit of Humphreys Peak as the winter abode of kachinas, elemental spirits, who visit their mesas during the growing season, carrying much-needed rain. In the plazas, the supernatural guests bestow blessings on the people during the seasonal cycle of dances and ceremonies. These mask bearers have even been known to cohabit with mortals, when the world was still rife with potential and magic.

A legend that was only fully recorded in 1980 links an account of how the Hopi first received water to the eruption of Sunset Crater. According to this tale, a young woman from Second Mesa, who had a reputation of being picky about suitors, was wooed by a Ka'nas kachina. The mysterious stranger quickly succeeded in melting her heart. On the back of a rainbow, which he flung from his sack of belongings, they traveled to his home on top of the San Francisco Mountains, to a place known as Cloud House. There, the girl had to prove her worth to his family.

In an ice cave near the summit, Hahay'iwuuti, the divine mother-in-law, tested the heroine's resolve and endurance for four consecutive days. While gales laid siege to the chilly chamber, she had to grind ice, hailstones, and icicles, instead of corn. The girl was repeatedly about to give in to fatigue and the blizzard's cold prowling; at some point, tears crystallized in the lashes of her eyes, sealing them shut.

But Spider Woman, who hid behind the girl's ear, helped with encouragement, as well as medicine herbs and magical turkey feathers that softened the ice on her grindstone. They also kept the shivering maiden from freezing to death. Each morning, Hahay'iwuuti entered the pit, surprised to find her daughter-in-law alive and the impossible chores completed. Each morning, she scooped all water from the grinding bin, gathering it in big-bellied earthenware jugs.

In the end, impressed by the girl's industry and courage, the kachinas welcomed her wholeheartedly into the family circle. Henceforth, her Ka'nas relatives would carry the liquid that had been collected and stored in countless vessels to the Hopi mesas, where it nourished the crops.

To get a better feeling for the terrain, and since the cone proper is now off-limits to hikers, I wander among cinder hills sprawling outside the monument boundaries. These "cinder dunes" are actually older volcanoes that have been blanketed with ejected material the size of peas and walnuts.

Climbing these coarser cousins of sand dunes is Sisyphean work. For every two steps uphill, I slide down one. Sinking ankle-deep in loose cinder and ash, I accumulate "trail mix" in my boots. The overlapping rhythms of my crunching steps and labored breathing splinter silence into more manageable parts. After only fifteen minutes of this, my thighs and lungs feel on fire. As if trudging at high altitude, I am forced to stop frequently. I catch my breath. I gulp water. I seek shade rather than sunlight to rest in—a sure sign that spring has again arrived in the desert. Hard to believe, that only last night, a membrane of ice grew on water left in my cooking pot.

Heat flimmers across the slopes. It hugs the ground closely, blurs contours in ascending waves; its weight presses hard on my shoulders. I pick up a snippet of lava ribbon, and it feels warm, as if it were still harboring heat from the volcano's intestines. Already on this April day, snow gleaming atop the San Francisco Peaks taunts with the promise of coolness. What I would give for a fistful of granular slush to suck on, or to press to my throbbing temples!

But the sights fully compensate for the suffering. Solitary pines and yellow-blooming cushions of bladder pod thrust through cinders that lack even traces of topsoil. From afar, bushes of withered Apache plume resemble tufts of blond fur clinging to balding skin. A pair of ravens tumble from the sky: now they dissolve against the black background. Now shadow twins chase them, darker than dark.

Descending the inclines is much more fun. I simply shift my weight on my heels and glissade down the steepness, raising a trail of dust.

❖❖❖❖

Like all stories, the legend of the Ka'nas kachina would taste flat without its share of villains and betrayal. After her trials atop the mountains, the Hopi girl who—unlike the deities—is never named in this tale, returned with her young husband to live on Second Mesa. As their household prospered, the couple incurred the envy of some villagers, who engaged in witchcraft. Plotting to divide them, one of the sorcerers, or "turds," disguised as her husband managed to seduce his wife during the kachina's absence. After she confessed to her spouse, he planned his revenge. To begin with, he withheld rain from the villagers, bringing down drought. To frighten the evildoers even more, Ka'naskatsina prepared a fire on top of a mound southwest of the mesas. His elders warned him against driving the fire pit too deep into the ground.

He then summoned Whirlwind from his home in a cavern. And with his help, some pitch, dry bark, and a piece of flint, a fire was started. But it soon leapt out of control, burning downward into the mound. Without hesitation, it merged with flames tended underground by relatives of Masau'u, god of fire and death.

The fire reared up and raced for the distant mesas, from where it was easily spotted. Ka'naskatsina and his relatives re-treated to a hill to the north, possibly O'Leary Peak. From there they observed the devastation. The red beast savaged grasslands and forests, while glowing snakes of lava inched toward the un-friendly villagers.

Aghast at the terror he had struck in the hearts of the Hopi, the youth eventually relented. He decided that a lesson had been taught. He fetched the wind one more time. Together they ran along the edge of the burn, herding the flames back where they had come from. When the blaze had died off, the land lay trans-formed. But order was far from restored; the kachinas were still holding a grudge.

❄❄❄

Although the first phase of volcanic activity had the greatest impact on the Sinagua, the molding of the landscape continued. Any exploring parties, sent from the nearby proto-Puebloan hamlet of Wupatki to see if the valley was fit to be settled again, would have witnessed massive lava flows (the Kana-a and Bonito flow) breaching the base of the crater in 1150 A.D. and 1220 A.D.

At the visitor center, I stroll through displays of the land's violent birthing. In squeeze-ups, pasty lava has been pressed through cracks, whose jagged jaws left grooves in the cooling slabs. Chunks of obsidian—dense, glassy lava rich in silica, and rapidly cooled—were coveted trade items for pre-Columbian residents, who fashioned arrow- and spearheads from it. Frothy volcanic glass hardened into balls of pumice instead. Next to it on the shelf sits a large gob that remained viscous longer, while airborne. This "bomb" could easily be mistaken for the petrified thigh muscle of a Greek hero.

The Hawaiian language provides terms for further variations on a common theme. Like *aa* or clinker lava, rubble fused in the melt-down; *pahoehoe* or rope lava, on the other hand, contains more gas. It flows in sheets that can be wrinkled or smooth as snakeskin. Many of these forms strike me as almost organic and invite tactile exploration.

Where the paved park road borders the two square miles of Bonito Flow near the foot of the cone, I admire more features, in place. A circular foundation is all that remains of a spatter cone or fumarole. Imprints of deliberately placed corn ears were found in lumps of cooled lava near similar gas vents, hinting at offerings to placate a short-tempered god.

Stunted aspen fringe the volcanic field, whose depth ranges from six to one hundred feet. In smoothness that blinds, trunks stand white and collected against gunmetal-gray-to-anthracite chaos. Bonito Flow is a textbook example of primary plant succession in the wake of natural disturbance. Splotches of pale green, neon yellow, and orange lichen encrust the serrated debris. Breaking down rock, they create a semblance of soil. A few ponderosas have gained footholds on top of the flow. On this highway from hell, blades of lava stand tilted, too close to place as much as a foot in between. I try to walk it nevertheless—and sound like a blind man groping around in ruins.

A sinkhole opens the ceiling of a cavity shaped like a tube. The dense material of the roof helps to insulate cold air trapped in its innards. Inside, I find relief from the parched surface and the sun's fervor. Slowly my eyes adjust to half-light, my skin to meat locker temperatures. Metal bars prevent further passage. They ensure the safety of visitors and—I suspect—the sanctity of the place. The Hopi consider this the lair of the North Wind. According to traditional belief, it is dangerous and forbidden to enter these kinds of places, but one may do so by appeasing and calming the genius loci, by speaking its sacred name. What times, when even gods find the doors to their homes padlocked against the ignorant!

I press my face against the cool grate. On its far side, ice lenses collect a residue of light from the entrance. One crevice holds an immaculate prayer stick: ochre, with its tip painted turquoise.

The higher powers had not yet doled out their full allotment of hardship to the wayward Hopi. Almost as an afterthought to Ka'naskatsina's wrath, the weather turned vicious. Another drought choked the land. One year, the corn withered on its stalks. It only rained once the entire summer. The following year, hailstorms that lasted eight days and eight nights wasted the crops. They even damaged some houses. Winters were much too dry, albeit riven by blizzards; summer gales stripped fields of their soil, or suffocated young corn under dunes. Famine ensued after all food stores had been depleted. First, people ate dogs, cats, and mice. Then, they added grasshoppers, cicadas, prairie dogs, and prickly pear cactus pads to the menu. Toward the end, a few hollow-eyed souls even devoured the skin coverings of drums, after boiling them. Squabbling and looting and theft became part of daily life. Of those who did not perish, many left the area, seeking better lives elsewhere.

Harold S. Colton, the leading researcher of the Sinagua in the Flagstaff vicinity, advanced a "land rush hypothesis" in the 1930s, to explain changes in the archaeological record. He attempted to link post-eruptive population increases and the cultural flourishing evidenced in a communal pueblo and ball court at Wupatki, with improved farming conditions. Colton proposed that the Sinagua actually benefited from a thin layer of cinder scatter. Loose and porous, this mulch absorbs rainfall and snowmelt; it reduces runoff and evaporation. It promotes tree growth at lower elevations as well. In addition, the black cover stores the sun's heat, lengthening a growing season that is precariously short at these elevations. According to Colton, strong winds later clogged springs and bared already marginal soils of their cinder mulch. This accelerated the abandonment of a region, which lay depopulated by the end of the thirteenth century.

More recent studies seem to contradict some of Colton's assumptions. Local rather than regional horticulture did indeed benefit from moderate cinder fall. But civilizations also evolved outside the impacted area, and other factors have to be held responsible. Pollen and tree ring analysis for example, shows that a blossoming of the Sinagua and Ancestral Puebloan cultures at large was accompanied by warmer and moister periods, interrupted by drought episodes between 1066 A.D. and 1130 A.D.

The onset of cooler and drier conditions throughout the Southwest after 1250 A.D. generally reduced arable land on the Colorado Plateau. Commonly known as the Little Ice Age, this trend not only doomed the Norse colony in Greenland, but also sufficiently explains the demise of the pre-Columbian peoples of the Four Corners region.

Could it be merely coincidence that tribal memories of these upheavals verify a sequence of cultural and climatic changes postulated by modern science? The legendary account of weather escapades, of drought, severe erosion, civil disturbance, and outmigration, matches scientific narratives that are based on sophisticated research. In a recent approach in anthropology, oral traditions are not only consulted to corroborate data obtained from the geosciences, but also to gain new insights.

Satisfying a human craving for closure, the legend of the vengeful deities has a happy, if somewhat anticlimactic, ending. The kachinas relented eventually. Harmony was restored in the village as well as the universe, and after a sumptuous banquet on Second Mesa, with food provided by a procession of gods decked out in feathers and furs, conditions began to improve. Life became as normal as it ever can be in a desert place.

A West Coast screenwriter scripted yet another plot involving Sunset Crater. It shattered the eggshell appearance of normalcy once again. The sleepy town of Flagstaff was buzzing in 1928, aroused by plans to blow up the cone. This time, mortals would be responsible. This time, TNT instead of magma would do the job.

The Famous Players - Lasky "Moving Picture" Corporation was going to shoot an adaptation of Zane Grey's novel *Avalanche*. All they needed for a sure blockbuster was a landslide. Harold Colton, eminent researcher and founder of the

Museum of Northern Arizona, got wind of the planned special effects. He fought for "his" ruins and the crater, aided by the U.S. Forest Service and local citizens. Eventually, one of the earliest environmental grassroots movements in the West succeeded in 1930, when President Herbert Hoover signed Sunset Crater Volcano National Monument into existence.

Its archaeological and volcanic treasures have so far been preserved for posterity. Yet cinder cones outside the sanctuary are still threatened: off-road vehicles (ORVs) mar some of the naked flanks, while others are gutted for landscaping and building material, and to "salt" icy roads.

The main reason I walk these bleak fields is, however, not Hollywood's folly. Neither is it the subterranean violence unleashed by gods or volcanoes. No, I have come above all for the pink penstemon, which graces this moonscape with splashes of color.

I don't have to look hard to find specimens. A cluster of them grows right next to the visitor center. The leaves are arranged in pairs—serrated, still curled, and edged in burgundy. They fuse at the base, tenderly clasping the long flower stalks. The plants still lack their glorious blossoms, but a few more weeks of warmth and a good dousing or two will bring them to life. Soon, dozens of pink mouths will wag red tongues, calling out to hungry hummingbirds.

What is this flower's attraction? Certainly not a temporary listing with other endangered species. Nor did its uniqueness draw me, the flowery thumbprint of evolution that singles this place out from all others. *Penstemon clutei* is endemic to the monument. It occurs nowhere outside of this closely circumscribed niche. Like Darwin's finches, this many-throated miracle confronts us with a rather recent case of adaptation. Deviating from all other members of the figwort family, this one adjusted to a radically changed world.

As usual, I feel most deeply affected by the power of the sublime, by the incarnation of meaning in leaf and stem and root. In a humble reversion of the law of minuscule causes and great effects, a cataclysm reverberates through centuries or millennia and brings forth something as temporary, yet timeless, as a fragile pink flower.

The Victorian botanist Richard Deakin expressed this very same sentiment, while inventorying the flora inside the ruins of Rome's Coliseum. "Flowers form a link in the memory and teach us hopeful and soothing lessons amid the sadness of bygone ages," he felt. And, "cold indeed must be the heart that does not respond to their silent appeal; for though without speech they tell us of the regenerating power which animates the dust."

Back on the highway that cuts through the volcanic field, I turn for a last look at the monument. Gray clouds have drifted down from the San Francisco Peaks. One blooms straight above Sunset Crater, resembling a plume of ash.

## 2

# BEELZEBUB'S WEEKEND RETREAT

*"Know then, O waiting and compassionate
soul, that is to fear which has the power to
harm, and nothing else is fearful even in Hell."*

—Dante Alighieri,
*The Divine Comedy,* Canto II

I TRAIL THE GUTTED ROAD THAT BOUNCES TO THE SANDY BOTTOM
of Devils Canyon. The gorge burrows through the uplift of the
San Rafael Swell, roughly on an east-west axis. Its south-facing
walls have already been licked clean by the eager sun of late winter, revealing golden sandstone capped with pastry layers of the
Carmel formation. The north-facing slopes in the shade look like
a different canyon, a different season altogether. They are still
flecked with rags of snow, right down to the threadbare wash.

Nests of white fluff in the creek bed remind me of down
from the wings of a fallen angel. (Evidence of Lucifer's plunge?)
Upon closer inspection, they turn out to be clumps of mountain
mahogany seeds. Each seed sports a feathery tail. These miniature sails help the bush spread its progeny on the wind. When I
glance around, I spot the indomitable evergreens scattered across
the slopes above.

✧✧✧

Like all lovers, I am curious and care deeply about names for the beloved. In the naming of shrubs and birds, rock and cloud formations, places, the world appears holy and whole again. A flotsam of associations, stories, dreams, and meanings—even hopes—snags in the net of names we have cast upon this earth. It differentiates anonymous space into familiar, lived-in places. A scatter of names distinguishes every place from every other place. It creates the vocabulary of belonging that roots each one of us in this world.

For quite some time, I had been puzzled by a profusion of diabolical monikers incongruously slapped onto desert localities that for me approximate paradise. Maps of the Colorado Plateau intrigue me with dark names: Devil's Garden. Devil's Lane. Hell Hole Canyon. Devil's Chair. Hell's Backbone. Devil's Slide and Hell's Kitchen. Some, like Hell's Half-Mile, Satan's Gut, and Hell to Pay warn of boulder-spiked bottlenecks awash with whitewater. They also carry treasured memories of Moebius strip-days and wet roller coaster rides.

Initially I assumed these coinages were only manifestations of sheepherders' nightmares or early river runners' fears. I thought they reflected the disdain pioneers and explorers, weaned on pastoral eastern landscapes, felt for an alien land puckered with heat. In historical accounts not exclusively referring to the American Southwest, the desert has been depicted as the abode of howling demons. Monsters dwell here. Wild beasts. Half-naked savages. Deluded hermits. Prophets and saints retreated here from the world—only to find their flesh shrivel as a foretaste of hell, to be tempted by Satan's desiccating lies. The "red devils" and "heathens," who roam these parts, keep rearing their ugly heads throughout the journals of settlers who feared god, wild things, and disorder more than death. Conquistadors christened parts of this hardscrabble *el mal país*: "the bad land." And Indian fighter General Phil Sheridan quipped that if he owned hell and Texas, he would rent out Texas and go live in hell.

Perhaps the skin-searing climate ignites imaginations, or the glow of red rocks under an infernal sun. Some may mistake dust devils that reel across blistered plains for evil spirits, the stink of rotten eggs emanating from certain springs for the Antichrist's perfume. Cloven hoof prints in the wet sand of a wash may be nothing but tracks of cattle and mule deer. And yet.

Some of the most heartily disliked plants of the Southwest contribute to the reputation of these badlands. Thorns of the catclaw acacia shred clothes and flesh of the careless rider, and led to the invention of leather chaps. If need be, steel fishhooks can be replaced with the curved barbs from the devil's-head or barrel cactus. (Not that too many people carry fishing tackle out here.) And even the harmless seedpods of the devil's claw or unicorn plant resemble parasitic creatures from outer space.

Horned shaman figures pecked into boulders by pre-Columbian hunters always seem to be watching; their presence does not help either to make the ignorant or susceptible feel at ease. Even contemporary rhetoric is not free of bias. In many books, and much film and news coverage, the desert is reviled as a hostile, if not hellish, environment. These days, the unholy host seems to come dressed in checkered Palestinian head scarves and desert fatigues.

As I learned more about these flinty wastes and arroyos, I realized that the issue was far more complex: for every Dirty Devil there seemed to be a Virgin River, for every Hellroaring Canyon an Angel's Landing. What I witnessed was a morality play staged against a backdrop of mesas, gulches, playas, and buttes. Early colonists, who were not always of an unflinching religious disposition, simply projected one of the most fundamental human dramas onto the seemingly blank screen of this obstinate landscape: the struggle between light and dark, between good and evil. Even Native Americans, whose bones have mingled with this dust so much longer than ours, identify places of evil, witchcraft, and sorcery amid their sacred geography.

The—often cataclysmic—processes that shaped these barrens are laid bare in the unease of their geology. Meteor craters pock the desert skin. Salt domes swell and burst like ulcers. Jagged canyons scar the tissue of the earth, and the cores of extinct volcanoes stick like scrawny necks from salt plains. Fault lines break open hundreds of miles of rock crust, resembling sharks' teeth, gigantic cockscombs, or the backbones of mythical beasts. Rock strata have been tilted, crumpled, and torn. They appear torched and—littered with boulders—as the battlefields of long-vanished races of titans.

One may consider such notions naïve, romantic, or anthropocentric. But I believe that a metaphorical connection with the earth is preferable to no connection at all. Or to a strictly utilitarian one that opens doors for exploitation and rape.

When I looked deeper into the iconography of place-names, I began to see patterns. Even the most perfunctory use of a collection of Utah place-names shows the minions of hell outnumbering angels by at least two to one. It seems that we are obsessed with the malevolent and rather bored by saintliness. Violence and moral depravity are the standard fare of our evening news and tabloids. And except for one listing, paradise is exclusively located in the relative lushness of northern Utah's Uinta Mountains. Quite tellingly, the origin of "paradise" can be found in the Old Persian words *pairi* ("around") and *daæza* ("enclosure"), describing a walled-off garden. In this version of Eden, anything wild and unkempt is to be kept out, to protect the human dream of order against nature's infinite law—chaos.

A good number of the "heavenly" places owe their names to Hispanic explorers. They either honored the Virgin Mary (Zion's Virgin River and bastardized Verkin Creek), or their patron saints (like San Raphael and San Juan). They established sanctuaries. They pleaded for safe passage through the unknown.

English place-names seem to have become attached to complementary categories of landmarks: angels seem generally to be associated with lofty roosts, headlands; gracile arches, as well as springs, trails, and coves form celestial refuges from the wilderness. Angel Cove, a spring-fed, lush alcove in the Dirty Devil drainage, is just one example. The Archenemy, on the other hand, owns real estate in the form of forbidding canyons. He rules from subterranean chambers and mazes of bizarre rock formations. Hell'n Maria Canyon near the Wyoming state line appears to be the only neutral ground where good and evil meet and can probably be excused as the slip of a heat-crazed, blaspheming prospector.

Every person has his own vision of hell. For some it happens to include lava fields and tinder cones baked by earth fire and midsummer heat. For myself, the place of eternal damnation comes fully furnished with neon-lit office cubicles, rush hour, hospital corridors, fifty different brands of toothpaste, tax forms, Rush Limbaugh and Jerry Springer, Wal-Mart, Burger King, celebrity autobiographies...and off-road vehicles.

The bottom of Eagle Canyon, from which I crossed over, had been marred by snarls of tire tracks cutting into sparse vegetation. But piles of horse manure in varying degrees of freshness assure me that Devils Canyon has not yet been discovered by wheeled weekend hordes.

Near its mouth, large patches of biological soil crust (formerly known as cryptobiotic soil) carpet the ground. Undisturbed, they keep the topsoil in place. Fungi, cyanobacteria, lichens, mosses, and wind-blown spores form a living, breathing, digesting community of micro- and macroscopic life that crenellates and enriches the earth. The brittle veneer converts and fixes nitrogen and carbon, the most important nutrients in this environment. According to Jayne Belnap, a research ecologist with the U.S. Geological Survey, it constitutes the true bottom of the desert food chain. The knobby surface acts as a sponge, absorbing and retaining rainwater, up to ten times its own volume. This secretive life form is easily crushed by boot, hoof, or fat tire and takes decades or even centuries for its recovery. To the uninitiated, it looks like plain dirt.

Devils Canyon has been designated a Wilderness Study Area (WSA) by the Bureau of Land Management (BLM), which means it is under consideration for selection as protected wilderness. But I know that this in itself does not necessarily guarantee its integrity. Too often, WSA boundary markers become a substitute target of aggression. Vandalized and scattered about, they are the unmistakable calling cards of motorized fun pigs, out to kick up some dust. Perhaps not all backcountry motorists behave like dirt-road warriors. But land managers, concerned citizens, and conservation groups report frequent disregard for road closures, private property, and trail restrictions. Having a powerful machine as an extension of one's physical prowess simply seems to call forth the inner barbarian: even an ATV-industry poll showed that "more than half of the respondents had used their machines to trespass illegally."

Resource extraction and recreational abuse can become promiscuous bedfellows. Associations of motorists clamoring for unrestricted access to public lands not only receive funding from vehicle manufacturers like Honda and Kawasaki; corporations like Marathon Oil and Crown Butte Mines also provide financial backup. Another sponsor—the Louisiana-Pacific Corporation—owned a pulp mill operation and contributed to the clear-cutting of southeast Alaska's Tongass National Forest.

Though not always readily apparent, an insidious union of interests known as the "Wise Use" movement hinders efforts to preserve public lands. Motorized use of wild places may become established in as little as a decade or less, with or without official approval. Where that happens, federal agencies become unwilling to recommend wilderness designations. More lenient management prescriptions keep these impacted areas "available"—until earthmovers and dozers and drilling rigs are ready to finish them off.

Conservation organizations have sued the bureau repeatedly, for turning too many blind eyes on violations. But the agency is also chronically short on dedicated field personnel who could prevent the bulldozing of new county roads, the uprooting of WSA markers, or the removal of BLM road barriers.

Many rural residents see the federal government's "locking up" of public lands in wilderness areas as meddling with state sovereignty. These feelings sparked the Sagebrush Rebellion whose fires are still fed by misinformation and the hope for quick profits. A recent motion to declare the San Rafael Swell a national monument was foiled by local pro-development factions, supported by ORV organizations, and politicians afraid of alienating their constituencies.

Following missionaries, ranchers, and prospectors, off-roaders are only the latest and least hardy in a succession of people staking their claims: the recreational tearing-up of the desert started in the 1950s. Initially, fans of the American outback and rock hounds in army surplus jeeps took to old mining roads to scout remote canyons and mesas. In the 1960s, however, with the advent of dirt bikes independent of even the most marginal tracks, driving became an end in itself. "4x4" became a magical formula. "Hill-climbing," the monotonous up-and-down riding of steep hills and sand dunes, is still the ultimate high. At present, due to the BLM's interpretation of its multiple-use mandate, only five percent of the lands included in the Redrock Wilderness proposal are closed to off-road abuse. Utah is second only to California in the grinding to dust of fragile desert flora and fauna.

A single boot print in a creek bed promises the quiet company of fellow desert rats. It promises a hushed exchange of information about springs, routes, wildlife sightings, a sharing of favorite haunts. The parallel incisions of four-wheelers on a Morrison butte on the other hand, unfailingly announce obnoxious exhaust, bonfires, shooting contests, and noisy partying, shattered dreams of silence and solitude.

Among the environmental costs of this gas-guzzling, land-gobbling nonsense is the destruction of vegetation and wildlife; damage to archaeological sites; spiraling erosion; compacted soils, and fouled water sources. Shrubbery broken by tires no longer provides food, shelter, shade, or nesting material for desert dwellers. ORVs collapse the burrows of prairie dogs. They crush the nests and tunnels of other subterranean residents. In Nevada desert tortoises are mangled by the dozens, barely hanging on to the endangered species list. Research has shown that the racket causes kangaroo rats to bleed from their ears; half deaf, they run around frantically, with increased heart rates and metabolism. Fringe-toed lizards and desert iguanas have been known to lose their hearing completely. But a keen sense of hearing is essential for the survival of many species in an environment where cover is scarce: animals rely upon it to locate or avoid becoming prey, to find mates, establish territories, and navigate. Whenever possible, they give noisy areas a wide berth.

During late summer, spadefoot toads get ready to leave their burrows. They are hardwired to mate and lay eggs, to seek moisture and take advantage of a narrow window of opportunity. Deluded by the false rumblings of ORVs, which they mistake for the first growling of thunderstorms, they emerge prematurely—only to face desiccation and death.

Soil compaction in tracks, caused by as little as a single vehicle, keeps rain from fully percolating through surface layers. The resulting runoff scrapes out gullies that foster further downcutting and hillside erosion. A single day's joyride has thus the potential to create effects still visible to the rider's grandchild. Increased soil temperature and the diminished cycling of nutrients are additional consequences. Unburned fuel seeps into groundwater. Frequently binding to soils, it accumulates and can persist for years.

I cannot help but wonder if calloused attitudes toward this desert fastness are perhaps leftovers from the old Wagons West mentality: a person sealed off in his air-conditioned, horse-powered steel box perceives nothing but obstacles that need to be overcome. Hurdles need to be taken without popping a tire or busting an axle. Once again, men and their machines are pitted against wild nature.

The backpacker, however, appears to be much more attuned to the landscape. He (and, unlike in off-roading, equally often "she") beds down for the night on naked ground. He curls into the shade of a boulder. Sips from a pothole and flames of a fire from dead juniper twigs equally nourish his body. When clouds pull a veil of gauze across the remorseless sun, the weary soul rejoices, and opens for the nurturing spirit of this place.

There is a narrow neck of land separating two canyons nearby. It is labeled Devils Racetrack on my BLM map. Wrong place! These tortured washes are Satan's *real* playpens, marked by the zigzag spoor of rubber thread and the stench of diesel fumes. The dusky skin of the desert deserves to be treaded on lightly, individually and on foot—if at all.

Speed distorts perception. Noise prevents contemplation. Infernal combustion leads to obesity. The average American these days walks a mile and a half per week. That is "walking," not "hiking." This includes forays to the bathroom and garage, daring explorations of the corner store and bank. And since I even walk three or four miles when in town, there must be quite a few fellows out there who ambulate considerably less than their three hundred fifty yards each day.

The annual Jeep "Safari" in Moab draws thousands of thrill seekers. Caravans of forty or more ORVs and SUVs and ATVs, and increasing numbers of Humvees, grind their way over slickrock and slash through blackbrush flats. Occasionally, a vehicle flips on its back and lies helpless like a grounded beetle. Organizations like the Southern Utah Wilderness Alliance are taking on the devil-may-care attitude of many "festival" participants, but when they request that jeepers stay on designated trails, activists are likely to be told to go to hell. If these rugged individualists knew what they are missing, they might forego cushioned seats once in a while.

My acuity of vision increases as I slow down in the backcountry. I notice minute details, pull them into focus as I walk. An observer speeding at "the velocity of glimpses" is only likely to register general appearances.

In one of my proudest feats as an outdoorsman, I once identified a canyon by its scent alone. We were floating through lower Cataract Canyon, and the night was overcast, as dark as it can only be at the bottom of a gorge. Bone-tired, we wanted to pull over at the mouth of Dark Canyon, for a few hours of sleep. Each gap in the darkness looked like our tributary. I had hiked Dark Canyon before and remembered a tangle of sacred datura near its mouth. Sure enough, a breeze soon carried the sultry, unmistakable perfume of moonflower blossoms to our rafts.

The way to intimacy of perception is to toss your car keys. Lace up your boots and regain a pedestrian purity. Reclaim the openness of a toddler's first encounter with the world! It works equally well for touch, smell, and hearing, and each newly awakened sense will sharpen your awareness exponentially. The Japanese call this "seeing with the eyes of the heart."

It is hard on this crisp day to find a campsite where the ground has thawed enough to receive my tent stakes. I finally succeed on a bench of loose sand. Cliff flanks reverberate with the muted droning of cars on the interstate, which grazes the Swell less than a mile away. Sound waves slide down escarpments. They clog the canyon bottom and engulf my island camp in a slowly rising flood. They create an aural distortion, diminishing the illusion of unlimited space that is the hallmark of true wilderness. "Hell is other people," wrote Jean-Paul Sartre, and even out here, it can be.

Only rarely do we stop to think. Only rarely do we classify noise within the same category as roads, power lines, dams, and barbed-wire fences. We filter it from our perceptions, which become selective, a skill acquired early in life, in the humdrum of cities. But just as the visible lines we lay on the land limit personal space, white noise surrounds us with impenetrable walls.

A seep I was counting on for water turns out to be solid. Hell *has* frozen over, yet no snow can be found in this part of the canyon. Luckily, icicles sprout from an undercut, like stalactites in a cave. I fill my jug with daggers of opaque ice. While they melt on my camp stove, I stare into its corona of blue hissing flames. My thoughts shift to an encounter near the brink of this canyon, a few days ago.

I had been daydreaming, lulled by the repetitive crunching of my steps in the snow. As I drifted among pinyon and juniper dwarves, a sudden blur jolted me back into reality: feathers-yellow-legs-talons-a-bright-rump-spot. A northern harrier had swept in on a flock of juncos, which were gleaning the white crust of edible morsels, as unaware as myself. The raptor failed to score, quite possibly distracted by my appearance.

Almost immediately, I felt a connection. For an instant, foreign lives focused on different agendas had awakened to each other's presence. Like lightning, I had cut into the intimate dance of life and death. I had been admitted to the inner sanctum that is so much more real out here than the muted spectacle of TV news, papers, and police blotters. Freed from the need for moral judgment, I stood galvanized between these creatures, sensing the beauty of necessity, as if for the first time.

As I hunker in front of my stove, I now realize that the desert is neither evil nor benign. It simply exists. It exists apart from our categories and archetypes. The flash flood taking your life does not care one iota; neither do rocks, cacti, or coyotes. We imbue the land with devils and angels that ride on our shoulders, whispering seductively into our ears. We carry them wherever we go. And a world that does not care is scarier by far, than a world ruled by evil.

I have looked carefully for signs of the fiend in this canyon. But short of the pus-colored, bloated discharge from a distant coal-burning power plant, I have not even seen the tip of his tail.

# 3

# SPLENDID DESOLATION

*"Floating the rivers takes you through the land, not merely over its surface. Entering a canyon is akin to entering the living body of the earth, floating with its lifeblood through arteries and veins of rock, tuning your perceptions to the slow pulse of the land, single beats of river current marking the steady rhythmic changes in geologic time. This particular form of intimacy...can only be had on the rivers. It flows through your memory and leaves behind a ripple of emotion: reverence."*

—Stephen Trimble,
photographer and writer

MOSQUITO WAS A STRANGER WHO CAME TO THE UTE ONE day, carrying two bags on his back. He promised the people to open these and to distribute his goods among them, at a calm place in the mountains. When they all had assembled there, he untied the bags. Dark clouds of mosquitoes poured forth, killing everybody. A neighboring band heard of this, tracked him down, and burned him and his vile bags on a big fire of sagebrush. A few mosquitoes escaped, multiplying vigorously, but fires of sage are to this day used to keep the foe at bay.

I am camped on a sandbank backed by an inscrutable gallery forest of tamarisks. The silty water of the Green River roils silently at my feet. My hands and face are covered with welts from the bloodthirsty insects that escaped the wrath of the Ute. The low water of midsummer has bared sandbanks and muddy shorelines, providing excellent breeding grounds for my tormentors. Outside of the tourist season, they live off other warm-blooded animals and, in the absence of these, suck plant juices from willow leaves and grasses. For their reproduction, however, females depend on the red sap of life.

I experience Desolation Canyon as it was seen for the first time and ought to be seen: from a boat.

In 1869 Major John Wesley Powell launched a first expedition at Green River, Wyoming, consisting of four wooden boats, his brother, and a crew of eight ex-soldiers and mountain men. He completed the daunting descent four months later at the mouth of the Grand Canyon in Arizona; only six men in two boats were flushed out of the lower gorge. They were greeted by two Mormons and a Paiute, who were looking for wreckage from the expedition. Rumors that the Colorado River disappeared underground for a stretch of its canyon fortunately proved to be false. Until that time, the thirty-four-year-old professor of geology who had lost an arm in the battle of Shiloh had never been to this desert. But he fell for it hard and fast, returning for a second voyage two years later.

His report on the geology, geography, and natural history of the Colorado and Green Rivers already included candid recommendations against dense settlement of the arid Colorado Plateau west of the hundredth meridian. But droves of land-hungry settlers flocked to the desert, believing that rain would inevitably follow the plow. Disenchanted with this development, Powell moved on and became the head of the newly founded Bureau of Ethnography, a government institution dedicated to the documentation of Native American cultures. Together with the journals kept by some of his crew members, his account offers first glimpses of the most remote area in the continental United States. It still stands as a vivid document of scientific curiosity, human daring and endurance.

In the wake of the one-armed explorer I push my raft into the sluggish current, glad to escape the whining bloodsuckers on shore. Almost immediately, I fall into the rhythm of rowing, which, like all monotonous physical labor, soon becomes automatic. It frees the mind to absorb its surroundings, to blend with the consciousness of the canyon. Shady campsites float by. Rock art panels lie half-hidden behind thickets of reed, box elder, squaw bush, coyote willow, and tamarisk dusted with pink blossoms. Cliff swallows' nests stick to the ceilings of overhangs gouged from banded canyon walls through millennia. A flock of these metallic-black birds sips delicately from the shallows, wings madly aflutter. There is a Pueblo Indian legend that the first people learned to plaster their buildings by watching swallows construct spherical homes from river mud baked in the sun.

I glide through the rotunda of Sumner's Amphitheater. Staircase buttresses radiate from the outside of the river meander like spokes of a wheel, and the Major himself observed how, "In these quiet curves vast amphitheaters are formed, now in vertical rocks, now in steps." He named this sweep of the river after one of his boatmen.

Unfortunately, the quiet curves could easily become festering sores, and noisy, if increasing energy demands and economic pressure would revive an interest in the unprotected canyon's oil shale. Locals have known about the existence of rich deposits—which are not true shale but rather organic marl—for quite some time. The Ute Indians of northwestern Colorado told of "mountains that burned," tales that were probably based on personal observations of oil shales ignited by lightning strikes. A settler in the same region built the chimney and fireplace of his homestead from the easily cut and locally abundant black rock. During a "housewarming" party, it caught fire, burning his log cabin to the ground.

The Green River formation is the result of deposits from rivers that emptied into ancient Lake Uinta, which covered tens of thousands of square miles during the Tertiary, about fifty million years ago. Clay and sand-sized particles and volcanic ashes washed into this lake. The runoff also enriched it with organic material—fish carcasses, leaves, stems, insects, and tree trunks. Some of this sedimentary matter has been transformed by pressure from overlying layers, as well as chemical processes, into carbon-based compounds. These include oil of various grades. The blocky layers of mudstone also encase a hoard of scientific treasures: beautifully preserved outlines of leaves and fish and other aquatic animals delicately trace the rocks. Near Stampede Flat I had stopped briefly, to marvel at a shield-like imprint of a turtle carapace atop a boulder. Its whorls stood out in their singularity, like a person's fingerprint.

These vast deposits could only be exploited in a complicated and costly process in which shale is strip-mined, crushed, and heated to about nine hundred degrees Fahrenheit to free mineral oil from the enclosing rock. One ton of shale would yield up to thirty gallons of oil; three and a half barrels of water would be required to mine just one barrel of black gold. The magnificence of this place would be soiled forever.

I listen to the creaking of oarlocks. Swirling vortices follow the dipping blades like miniature maelstroms. Overcome by noon heat and maudlin thoughts, I grab a beer from the cooler, lie down on my back, and let the current take me wherever it wants. As the boat slowly spins, a single cloud comes into view, floats to the periphery, and is gone. Long lines of broken cliffs, crags, and tower-shaped buttes circle around me. As if I were the center of *their* universe. The leaden warmth of the dog days and muted dripping from my shipped oars cause my eyelids to droop. A dragonfly lands on the bow. It seems no more inclined to work than I am. How different this lazy drifting is from the usual strenuous hiking, boulder hopping, and scrambling over bristling talus slopes.

But reading the river is not too different from route-finding on dry land. "Sleepers" are rocks that lurk barely below the surface, waiting to stall the careless boater, or to tear open the belly of a raft. Eddies and riffles, pourovers, hydraulics, and lateral waves need to be gauged and a trajectory chosen that requires the least amount of physical effort and yields the most fun. An elegant line through the rinse-and-spin cycle of rapids is something to be proud of. Part-time river runner and full-time monkey-wrencher Edward Abbey had it all figured out. He counseled, "A good boatman must know when to act, when to react and when to rest."

In the afternoon a fierce wind rears its head, blowing upriver, as it always seems to. It whistles in my oars. Tries to wrest them from my hands. I swing the raft around to use my stronger back-stroke, rather than pushing against the incoming tide. The current has turned to molasses. Ripples run through a swath of lush grass on a sandbank, swaying it like a field of wheat; an island of immaculate sand cradled between two limbs of the river seems to be smoking. Spray is whipped from whitecaps, making the water harder to decipher. Defeated, I pull out to camp on river right.

The inviting campsites on the opposite bank are off-limits, part of the Uintah–Ouray reservation of the Ute Indians established in 1868. Several divisions of this southern plains tribe were relocated to Utah after trouble erupted in Colorado in 1879, where white settlers once again coveted land that lay fallow.

An agency had been built right in the middle of the tribe's best grazing grounds. The Indians despised Nathan Meeker, the agent, who attempted to coerce these proud horsemen and buffalo hunters into farming. One sub-chief complained that his ponies were being cut up by the barbed wire that divided their pastures. Things came to a boil, when the agent ordered their horse race-track plowed under, and he was beaten by an enraged brave. Incensed, he sent for troops to guarantee his protection. At the same day, the approaching relief column was ambushed and besieged in a wagon fort. Another band of Ute warriors attacked the White River Agency and killed Meeker, by driving a stake through the mouth that had called for the end of a way of life. Six of his employees died with him, and his family was taken hostage.

More troops were sent in pursuit of the insurgents, who finally had to surrender. The White River and Uncompahgre bands were forced from their homelands and confined with their Uintah relatives under crowded conditions—the same old story sadly repeated throughout the West. During World War I, the government reclaimed more than eighty thousand acres of this reservation. Part of the newly assigned home was declared a naval oil reserve, to secure power for America's fleet of dreadnoughts.

After a luxurious dinner of grilled salmon and baked potatoes, I climb to a craggy promontory shouldering camp. A late party of boaters is still on the river. Like backswimmers, they stroke complacently down the gorge. Feathery cirrus clouds flare golden, then orange. They eventually fade to purple, while chocolate-brown canyon walls drown in shadows. Soon after, a silver-dollar moon transforms the rapids into crinkled aluminum foil.

The following day I land at the abandoned Rock Creek Ranch built by the two Seamounton brothers in the early 1900s. At this point Desolation Canyon out-gapes the Grand Canyon: five thousand feet from river to rim. Cascades of Douglas fir spill over the lip of the Tavaputs Plateau, plunging down rocky precipices. I cross a sun-baked pasture through the crepitating of grasshoppers that scatter under each step. Their palpitations mix with the pounding of blood in my ears. Away from the river's exhalations, the heat is oppressive, a good ten degrees higher. A side-blotched lizard scurries from rock shade to rock shade, leaving tiny zipper tracks in the sand.

Trout-bearing Rock Creek runs cold and idyllic. Lush foliage arches over a boulder-lined hole, suffusing the air with emerald glow. The crystal basin is deep enough to sit submerged. I ease in, soaking my sun-chafed body and sore mind.

The farmhouse of rough-hewn natural stone blocks is roofed with broad beams, and slowly falling apart. Quietly rusting implements strewn about the yard whisper of the hopes and dreams of people living at this remote frontier outpost. All tools and supplies had to be packed in on mule-back, down nearby Steer Ridge Canyon in the summer and upriver from Woodside during winter.

A chukar partridge struts in the shade of tall mulberry trees. The orchard's apple and apricot trees are heavy with fruit, but want pruning. Squirrels pelt the intruder with pits and half-eaten fruits, and when I start to retaliate, the obnoxious rodents protest with shrill jabbering. I relax against the solidity of a tree trunk and nibble on apricots, succumbing to their velvety sweetness. The muted roar of Rock Creek Rapid washes over the parched earth and me.

Back in the raft, I drift again; I cannot be bothered with rowing in this infernal heat. Canyon walls roll by like a film: crumbling, and insubstantial, dreams of a sultry summer day. Whenever I become too hot I jump overboard. I hook my feet under the chicken line and am dragged by my craft, kept afloat by the buoyancy of the life vest. With my body suspended in water, the day becomes weightless. Half asleep, lulled by lapping waves, I perk up at the sound of rapids ahead.

Periods of frenetic activity alternate with spells of lazing. I slip in and out of consciousness. Like the Taoist philosopher, I am unsure whether I am a man who has dreamt he was a butterfly or a butterfly who is still dreaming of being a man. Gradually, my skin darkens to the color of mahogany; my clothes have by now become almost unnecessary as protection against the sun. They are dull and stiff with river sediment. Days bleed into each other, like silt swirling in whirlpools, marked only by short explorations, or landfalls to camp for the night.

River time is real time. Prime time. Primal time. Only the flow of water and bodily rhythms determine the pace. At some point, baroque wigs of cumulus clouds pile up on the plateau, but rain never comes.

Eons or days later I pull out to scout thundering Coal Creek Rapid. This is the site of an attempt to domesticate the wildcat spirit of the Green River. In 1911 a crew of workmen began to excavate the foundations for Buell Dam here. A shaft in the bedrock and half-collapsed stone walls of a depot for explosives near the overlook of the rapids are the only remains. The project never proceeded beyond that phase. Lack of funding, as well as an unfavorable report by the U.S. Geological Survey regarding the quality of the underlying Mesa Verde Sandstone broke its back. My mind recoils at the thought that Desolation Canyon could have shared the dismal fate of Glen Canyon. With slack water backing up dozens of miles above a dam, the dreamscape of the past four days would have been inundated, lost in the twilight of progress.

Among rocks and the silvery bones of driftwood I find a dead swallowtail butterfly. Ants are slowly devouring its body. But the lemon-colored wings with black veins and a fringe of blue powder dots are still intact. With unease, I observe the spectacle of what I judge to be a voracious species consuming beauty, drawing facile and premature comparisons between them and us. Upon further thought, I have to acknowledge crucial differences. Unlike developers and bureaucrats intent on gutting the Colorado Plateau, these ants remain an integral part of the ecosystem. They are links in the chain of life. They recycle nutrients found in carrion; their subterranean cities and passages loosen and aerate arid soils. Their tunneling stands in stark contrast to our own endless diggings: it sustains rather than impoverishes this earth. It contributes to the great wealth that surrounds and carries each and every thing.

Terry Tempest Williams is a writer who has lamented loss of a different kind. She reflects on the stories that ally us with the land and each other, concluding "we can confront the mysteries of life directly by involving ourselves patiently and quietly in the day-to-day dramas of the land." Carefully, I pick up the dead butterfly, and it leaves smudges of stardust in my cupped hands.

# 4

# THIS OCCUPIED EARTH

*"Just as the land itself has shape and presence,*
*these place-names, tales and histories provide*
*both cultural contour and context to what cul-*
*tural geographer Estyn Evans would call 'the*
*occupied earth'."*

—Susan W. Fair, folklorist

## MATTHEWS PEAK—LUKACHUKAI MOUNTAINS

TO THE WEST, THE LAND FALLS OPEN LIKE A BOOK. THE SEVEN-thousand-foot-high Defiance Plateau slants toward distant Black Mesa; the weak chain of the Lukachukai, Tunicha, and Chuska ranges cannot quite cordon off its eastern edge. Silt-laden runoff from the western flanks of these mountains has gouged perpendicular gorges into the de Chelly Sandstone that show as flesh-colored cracks in the bulge. The abrasive sediment scooped out undercuts in which Ancestral Puebloan settlers found shelter. It also left alluvial bottoms fertile enough to grow corn, squash, beans, and, later on, fruit trees. Superb grazing along the rims, as well as perennial streamlets dashing from them made the twin canyons de Chelly and del Muerto comfortable places to live. Eventually, they became the last hold-outs of a nation under duress.

I have climbed up here for the view as much as for the history, or—to be more specific—for a view *into* history. An inveterate walker, I have always been fascinated by migrations of people. While it is relatively easy to comprehend the urge that sets an individual to wandering, the causes of mass movements seem far more complex. Yet like individual wanderlust, they reverberate far into past and future. Reading a landscape instead of a map provides a more intimate understanding of these callings, of the old pathways and routes. Walking them does so even more.

The land, which my eyes skim, is not wilderness, has not been wilderness for more than ten thousand years. It is storied. It is a palimpsest of a past that is still vibrant and inhabited. I am trying to understand the forces that pushed and pulled people across such rugged and dry terrain, creating their geography of fear and desire. The collective repository of these powers and resulting experiences are generally referred to as "history." There are as many histories as there are voices.

In Diné or Navajo culture, at least two complementary forms of history coexist. Both are alive in the spoken word. First, there are creation myths, explaining the origin of clans, customs, topographic features, the workings of a world that can never be fully understood, let alone controlled. These stories are sacred. Cyclical. Deep and rich as dark soil. They speak of events that occurred when humans were still able to communicate with animals; they speak of times when gods and goddesses walked the earth, shaping it as they went; visions and dreams and songs still had power; the border separating the real from the surreal was still open. The place of occurrence is far more important than the exact timing. This perspective strongly resembles Australian Aborigines' sense of a Dreamtime.

The second kind is the historical narrative or legend, often corroborated by non-native, written sources. These are secular tales. Their time frame is linear, shallow and one-dimensional. Unlike trickster myths—which are only told between first frost and first thaw, when thunder sleeps in its lair—they should be passed on only during the summer months.

Both genres can overlap and are equally important for Diné cultural and individual identity. By revisiting these stories, people embrace their origins and ascertain their place in creation. One should be cautious not to dismiss the mythic worldview light-handedly as "metaphorical," in favor of the seemingly literal interpretations of narratives that more closely resemble Western concepts of history. Storyteller Susan Straus points out ambiguity: "A myth is a true story that might never have happened, yet it reenacts itself in the lives of every human and in other living systems—including the land itself." Myths are nourished by archetypes that cut across cultural boundaries. They provide a subtext against which historical and personal tales find their fullest meaning.

I am camped on the flattened half-dome of Matthews Peak. This is Chézhin Náshjiní, or Lava-with-a-Black-Band-around-It, also known by a second, equally appropriate name—Tsé Binááyo'l'í— meaning Rock-around-Which-the-Wind-Blows.

To the north, the low saddle of Ayanií, or Buffalo Pass, dents basaltic escarpments dividing northeastern Arizona from northwestern New Mexico. The few gaps in this mountain fastness first admitted Diné onto the Defiance Plateau. Their enemies followed closely.

Buffalo Pass is an excellent example for the shimmering facets of history. Orthodox historiography explains the drifting of Navajo families from the Largo and Gobernador drainages of the San Juan River in northwestern New Mexico into Canyon de Chelly and Canyon del Muerto west of the Lukachukais with pressure from New Mexican settlers and pastoralists. It even dates the event: around 1750 A.D. A Diné myth sheds a different light on the pass, accounting for a different cause for migration. White Shell Woman, a Ye'ii or Holy Being, instructed the Navajo clans to disperse, but some became lost during their wanderings. Eventually, she appeared as a white buffalo, showing people the way across the divide.

I sit with my feet dangling over a lip of exposed mountain rump. Lava congealed rapidly here, pleating the cliff like a gigantic accordion. Defoliated scrub oak and aspen trees drift up to meet the foot of gray talus below. As far north as I can see, abutments of sandstone line the base of the Chuskas and Lukachukais; serrated edges and isolated buttes of pumpkin color evoke scenes from Monument Valley.

While I try to capture the view on paper, a solid mass of clouds begins pouring over the pass from the New Mexican side, blotting out anything below eight thousand feet. The ominous sea quickly engulfs the hamlet of Tsaile. It shrouds the plateau and washes silently against the base of the range. Only the highest promontories stay afloat, islands bronzed by a westerly sun.

A mob of ravens is tumbling in a dogfight, unconcerned that their world is being diminished each minute. They dive-bomb in and out of the advancing front. They shout hoarse encouragement to each other. Soon the rising tide overwhelms lower summits and ridges, wells up bare flanks, spills over and sweeps onward, as if on fast-forward. Through the occasional window, Tsaile Lake burns like melted silver.

Barely an hour after the start of this spectacle, the temperature plummets. The plume of my breath drifts with cloud rags, and I watch them catch in crags and pines that encircle my tent. Beyond a radius of one hundred feet, things—and perhaps time itself—have vanished. But the most amazing thing is the stillness of air: not a twig or pine needle stirs.

Later that night, I have to face the cold to relieve my bladder. I approach the abyss beyond the dimly outlined cliff carefully. Lights sparkle at my feet, like jewelers' wares spilled across black velvet. The hamlets of Tsaile, Many Farms, Round Rock, and Lukachukai lie in fierce competition with the glitter above. Coyote's laughter rises from the plains, a reminder of how those stars were first arranged.

In the beginning, the Holy Beings meticulously placed them in the night sky, outlining constellations: the Porcupine, Corn Beetle, Bear, the Horned Rattler. The male Big Dipper and its female counterpart, Cassiopeia, were set to chase each other around a campfire—the stationary North Star. The Ye'ii were taking their time, pondering how to position the gems still smoldering on a blanket at their feet. Coyote, who was watching the proceedings, became very frustrated, because they simply would not listen to his suggestions. In a surprise move he grabbed the blanket. He flung the remaining stars skyward, yipping and yodeling with glee. That is the reason why some are arranged in orderly fashion, while the rest appear to be scattered throughout space at random.

Ma'ii or Slim Trotter is historical personage, archetype, and demiurge rolled into one. He shaped this land, long before humans were even so much as a hazy thought in the mind of creation. Native people remember well that he stole for them from the gods: fire, tobacco, even daylight itself. But he also gave them mosquitoes and Death. It is in his nature. He cannot control it. Levity, gluttony, lewdness and rudeness, pompousness and mischief are all part of the parcel. He is buffoon, fringe dweller, shape-shifter, mythic prototype, and marginal existence. Like his disguises, his names are plentiful. Huddled in front of crackling flames, generations have reveled in the exploits of First Scolder—braggart, singer, punster, liar, and thief. In this manner people learned about right and wrong. They were reminded of how things came to be, and of the proper standards to live by.

He is also their contemporary, since new stories are added to ancient chronicles. Mythological time and modernity thus become linked. In memorable and hilarious encounters, he outsmarts traders, farmers, soldiers, whiskey peddlers, tourists, and show-offs—all those who don't know how to handle things wild and beyond control. Coyote finagles greedy Gray-eyes out of their horses and finery. He sells them gold-shitting asses, trees that grow money. He enjoys playing the defiant underdog, hero of the oppressed.

No single label seems to fit. I want to know who really hides under that ratty, flea-bitten coat. Perhaps nobody but my lost, dark brother, the shaggy shape that skulks through my dreams.

## NARBONA PASS—CHUSKA MOUNTAINS

It is simply impossible for me to resist another high point before descending to the Defiance Plateau. Outcroppings spattered with bile-green and yellow lichen flank a broad pass called Béésh Lích'íí Bigizh. The place is more widely known as Red Flint Summit. For a canyon rat who spends most of his time amid the palette of brittle sedimentary formations, the pewter solidity of basalt is a welcome change of scenery. Fragments of toffee-colored flint stone lie shattered between rocks. Before the introduction of iron, they were coveted for the chipping of arrow and spear points and provided the name for this pass.

Burly oaks and poised ponderosas have invaded the saddle. For a view, I have to climb a ridge and plateau to the south. From a spindly lookout tower that seems to sway in the calm, a panorama unfolds that makes my heart tingle.

Shiprock (Tsé Bít'a'í) bursts through the sere plain. Perfectly aligned with Sleeping Ute Mountain, it still betrays its birth from the liquid fire of earth's womb: the cooled eighteen-hundred-foot magma core of a blowout volcano was left standing, while the softer mantle surrounding the vent crumbled away.

But again, geology is only one of many potential frames of reference people use to satisfy their curiosity. The Rock-with-Wings is a holy place where Monster Slayer—a twin culture hero of Diné mythology—battled two cannibal gods in his quest to eradicate evil and make the earth habitable for humanity. One of the bird monsters snatched the creator-hero up in his talons, to feed him to its young. It dropped him near the nest, on a ledge of Tsé Bít'a'í. With arrows of sheet lightning, given to him by his sun father, Monster Slayer killed both parent birds, but instead of killing two orphaned nestlings as well, he swung the older four times around by the legs, directing that it should furnish bones and plumes for the people. This bird flapped away as a golden eagle. The younger one was twirled in the same manner and told that men would listen to its voice to learn of the future. This bird left the roost as an owl, preceded by a sinister reputation. And indeed, what greater threat than knowing the future could be envisioned?

Dibé Nitsaa or Big Sheep Mountain arches its white back above the flat haze of southwestern Colorado. On topographic maps it is called Mount Hesperus. The sacred mountain of the North stands as one of the pillars demarcating Diné Bikéyah, the ancient homeland of the People. Badlands beset the eastern horzon, eventually gentling on the slopes of Mount Taylor—Tsoodził — known to Diné as Blue Bead Mountain, sacred mountain of the South. This dormant volcano once spewed lava that can still be seen near Grants, New Mexico, and its coagulations are perceived as the dried blood of slain monsters.

The quartet of mountain shrines is complete with two summits that cannot be spotted from my perch. Dook'o'słííd or Mount Humphries in the San Francisco Peaks to the west, is where Light-Always-Glitters-on-Top. Last is Blanca Peak, in the Sangre de Cristo range. Sisnaajííní is forever Marked-by-a-Black-Horizontal-Belt.

Narbona Pass played a crucial role in "shallow" time as well, as a gate admitting enemies into the Land of the People. The conflict between the Spanish in New Mexico and the Diné has been attributed to characteristics typical of pastoralist societies. Driven by unchecked growth of their herds, native nomads and ranching colonists were forever doomed to expand overgrazed ranges and engage in spiraling warfare with competitors for the same resources.

By 1750, most Diné had acquired enough sheep to make the transition from a hunter-gatherer society to a people depending on gardening and herding. Horses served as currency in the trade with northern tribes still largely on foot; wild plant gathering and deer hunting on the blustery plateau and in the folds of the Chuska Mountains supplemented their livelihood. Serious raiding against New Mexicans commenced after 1753, when settlers pushed west along the Rio Puerco, occupying the best grazing ranges and water sources.

As governor of New Mexico from 1778 to 1788, Juan Bautista de Anza implemented a new Indian policy. It was founded upon the strict use of military force, the severing of native trade routes, and on playing tribes against each other—the old "divide and conquer" strategy. The dry lands became quickly embroiled. Comanche and Chiricahua Apache had formerly preyed on settlements of the Spaniards. Now they joined them to turn against the Diné, who were already battling their old nemesis, the Ute. Even inhabitants of the upper Rio Grande pueblos who had found refuge with the Diné after the Pueblo Revolt of 1680, now enlisted with the Spanish, leading them against their former hosts.

When New Mexicans settled around Mount Taylor, denying the Navajo use of pastures near Cebolleta, raiding and retributions spun out of control: Spanish irregular troops used Navajo depredations as excuses to conduct slaving expeditions. Their spoils of war fed booming silver mines and haciendas with cheap labor.

In a foray that was to set a pattern, Lieutenant Antonio Narbona marched in 1804 from Santa Fe by way of Laguna Pueblo, to pierce the Navajo heartland in the dead of winter. During that season families were relatively sedentary and congregated in their canyon hideouts. Somewhere in the blizzard-ridden Chuska Mountains, the motley militia of New Mexican and Sonoran dragoons and Opata Indian auxiliaries from Mexico lost their way. The invading host retreated to Laguna to regroup and recover, and to recruit guides from the Zuni pueblos.

In January 1805, three hundred troops eventually forced this pass, in yet another *entrada*. Once again, snow settled on their broad-brimmed black hats, but boot-length capes kept them from freezing. The breaths of horses and men mixed in the sharp air. Flintlock muskets were loaded and cocked, and rapiers glistened coldly in the winter glare, when they spurred their mounts toward Canyon del Muerto.

## MASSACRE CAVE—CANYON DEL MUERTO

On January 17, the column trailed Navajo tracks into the canyon. The soldiers of fortune laid waste to garden plots. They burned lodges and killed three hundred fifty goats and sheep. Alerted by their scouts, many Diné women, children, and elders and a few warriors had fled to a prepared cave high on the northern face of the cliffs. Most of the younger men were either off on a hunting trip in the Lukachukais, or on a raid of their own.

The hiding place is barely noticeable from the canyon bottom. According to one version, an old woman who had been a captive of New Mexicans could not contain herself. She started to hurl insults at the Spaniards, thereby revealing the refuge. After they had located the cliff shelter, the militia attempted to scale the steep slope. Valiant defenders poured arrows and rocks onto the ant-like figures below. The battle raged all day, and eventually Lieutenant Narbona sent a detachment to the rim of the canyon. From a flanking point these fusiliers poured lead into the alcove. Bullets ricocheted off the rear wall, and—mixed with flying rock splinters—mowed down Diné in a bloody harvest. In Narbona's own accounting, close to ten thousand rounds were fired that day.

Under such heavy fire, the assailants were finally able to gain the ledge, which could only be scaled with the help of pecked hand- and toeholds. Hand-to-hand combat ensued. A knife-wielding young woman grappled with a Spanish soldier in a macabre dance, and both fell more than six hundred feet to their deaths. According to oral tradition, blood streaked the sandstone cliffs crimson. People shoved each other over the edge, or jumped to avoid capture and enslavement. The name for the cave commemorates the day: Adah'aho'doo'nili̱ —Where-People-Were-Pushed-Down-from-a-Great-Height.

Estimates of casualties at the massacre site vary somewhat between 70 and 115. A number of women and children were taken away to become slaves in the upper Rio Grande settlements, and Narbona sent "eighty-four pairs of ears of as many warriors" to Santa Fe, as grisly proof of his "victory." But the count was most likely augmented with appendages cut from the heads of women and old men.

The difference, I hear, is hard to tell.

From a National Park Service overlook, I take in the scene of this drama. The only stains remaining on the face of the cliff are streaks of clay particles washed from the sandstone. No Diné ever set foot into the cave afterward, and as late as the 1970s human bones were supposedly piled behind boulders that formed the parapets. Holes from the hail of musket-balls still pitted the walls. "Collectors" had removed most of the skulls, however, and the oldest existing piece of Navajo weaving had been retrieved from the ossuary.

My gaze climbs several hundred feet of sheer rock separating talus from the embattled ledge. On this still autumn day, it is impossible to imagine the ferocity of the fighting, the desperation of women and children.

The Diné left a graphic record of this bleak time, above a rock ledge near Standing Cow Ruin. The Spanish Cavalcade Mural is an outstanding example of Navajo rock painting. Horsemen of the Narbona expedition prance across the wall, in details that are lively and crisp, down to brandished muskets, pigtail hairstyles, and the spotted coats of pinto horses. One rider's cloak is embroidered with the sign of the cross.

After Mexican independence in 1821, the wheels of conquest attempted to crush all opposition. Defense of the northern frontier fell to ragtag militias. The slave trade flourished, and the taking of captives became the driving force behind many incursions into enemy territory. Treaties were forged and broken. Reprisals took the form of costly punitive expeditions against the ever-elusive Navajo. Mexican forces had overextended themselves and were looking for allies to help bear the cost of protracted guerilla warfare. The preferred tactic was to stoke the fires of age-old antagonism between tribes. In spite of everything, the Diné grew into one of the wealthiest and most powerful tribes on the Colorado Plateau. But their inflated horse and sheep herds also left a legacy felt to this day. They contributed to erosion and the desertification of large areas. The government tried to curtail damage through drastic stock reductions in the 1930s and 1940s. Thousands of animals were slaughtered during this little-known intervention, creating painful memories—surpassed only by those of the Long Walk—that still linger in the mind of many an old-timer.

After the Mexican-American War of 1846, the U.S. government inherited two hundred years of hostility. With the treaty of Guadalupe Hidalgo in 1848, the burden to restore order throughout the ceded territories was passed on. The new realm included parts of Utah, Colorado, and New Mexico, plus all of California, Nevada, and Arizona. It was hard to police. Some Navajo mistook an initial policy of appeasement for a sign of weakness and were contemptuous of the new rulers of the land.

Narbona Pass became once more the gateway for an invasion of Diné Bikéyah, the heartland of the Diné to the west. In 1849, the new military governor of New Mexico, Lieutenant Colonel John Macrae Washington, launched a reconnaissance of the annexed domain. It was simultaneously meant as a show of force, to impress the rebellious subjects.

More than three hundred New Mexican volunteers from Jemez Pueblo joined almost two hundred regular troops of infantry, dragoons, and artillery. The combined forces were led by chief guide Antonio Sandoval, headman of a group of acculturated Diné who were considered renegades and outcasts by most of the tribe. After marching through daunting terrain near Chaco Canyon, this expedition rested in Tunicha Valley, east of the Chuskas.

There, Washington and the accompanying Indian agent conferred with some Diné leaders, including another Narbona—not his real name, but rather a moniker given to Hast'íí Naat'áni by the linguistically challenged intruders. The man named after the scourge of his people was a widely respected leader, agreeable to discussing a new and lasting peace. Unfortunately, the meeting came to a violent end that would shatter all trust and mark the beginning of two decades of bloodshed between the Navajo and the white-skinned Bilagáana.

A horse supposedly belonging to a Pueblo Indian scout for the army was spotted running with the Navajo herd. When Colonel Washington demanded the surrender of the animal and issued an ultimatum, the Diné negotiators left in a huff. The troops immediately opened fire with rifles and howitzers and seven warriors were left dead in the dust, including Narbona himself. Allegedly, the headman's scalp was taken. Two cartographers documenting the expedition later regretted not having been able to secure the entire head for "scientific" purposes.

The following day the party crossed the Chuska Mountains, replacing the Spanish lieutenant's name with a new one: Washington Pass. In spite of the treachery and atrocity of this encounter, two Diné leaders did sign a treaty near present-day Chinle. But the ink had barely dried, when a number of Rio Grande pueblos went up in flames: the Navajo had identified some Pueblo Indian scouts in the ranks of blue that fired volleys at Tunicha.

## NAVAJO FORTRESS ROCK—CANYON DEL MUERTO

At the junction of Black Rock Canyon and Canyon del Muerto, a steep-sided sandstone wedge broods, splitting one gorge into two. Its prow points down-canyon, toward the reservation town of Chinle. Although the hunkering mass appears to be an island, it is attached to the canyon's north rim by a low dam of natural rock. This is Tsélaa', Rock Tip, another place of hardship and suffering.

Under mounting pressure from the Ute, Pueblo Indians, U.S. troops, New Mexican settlers, and even Apache, Canyon de Chelly and its twin had been turned into crucial Navajo strongholds. A web of footpaths connected pastures and gardens. Runners scanned the horizon for dust clouds heralding the enemy. Cracks in the cliffs could hide warriors, women, and children, or else notched tree poles ascending to the rims. Scores of vertiginous hand- and toehold trails engineered by the ancients could be used like ladders without rungs, to escape to the plateau above. But the true pieces of resistance were half a dozen rock citadels strewn throughout the canyons.

It was the beginning of *nahondzod*—the Fearing Time.

The threat of a Confederate invasion of the Southwest had been averted at the price of lives at Valverde and Glorieta Pass. It was time for the Union army to turn its attention to "the Navajo problem" again. Brigadier General James Carleton, who had previous experience campaigning against the Navajo, assumed command of New Mexico in 1862.

Carleton was a hard-liner. He had been commissioned to study the tactics of European armies during the Crimean War and was greatly impressed by the strike-and-fade maneuvering of Russian Cossack units. He applied these lessons in relentless harassment to the Navajo. They were to be pursued without respite. They were to be kept on the move and prevented from following their seasonal round of subsistence and trade. Carleton would use a "scorched earth" strategy to bring these guerilla raiders into the fold of civilization. Winter, when Diné families were relatively stationary, and the lambing season of spring, were times of particular vulnerability.

In another farsighted move, Carleton appointed the retired Lieutenant Colonel Christopher "Kit" Carson commanding officer of the New Mexican volunteers. Long past his prime, Carson was already a living legend. Rope Thrower, some natives called him, for his handiness with the lariat. Many Diné knew him as Red Shirt. He had been freighter, trapper, trader, and guide throughout the Rocky Mountains and Great Plains for twenty years, before he began to scout for the military. Carson had long been the Indian agent and friend of the Ute. He had a working knowledge of Cheyenne, Arapaho, Crow, Blackfoot, Shoshone, Paiute, Ute, Comanche, Navajo, and Apache that served the army well.

In spite of his successes against the Jicarilla Apache and an invading Confederate column from Texas, Carson has been described as the antithesis of the career soldier. He was unpretentious, without formal education, but knowledgeable about all kinds of frontier lore, woodcraft, horsemanship, and terrain. At the time of his latest appointment, he was already fifty-three years old. He was also ailing from a riding injury.

The Ute scouts he brought with him complemented his many excellent skills. They were familiar with de Chelly's access routes from decades of raiding for livestock and slaves. A Ute named Grayhair, who was later killed by Navajo witchcraft, led these "Wolves for the Blue Soldiers." Each scout received blankets, food, tobacco, a rifle, saddle, and two horses in addition to whatever plunder he would secure. As leader of this band of citizen-soldiers and mercenaries, Carson was feared. He had even earned a certain amount of respect from the Diné, as a result of past encounters.

Bone-ravaging temperatures and six inches of snow hampered the troops as they left Fort Canby near present-day Window Rock in January of 1864. Before they reached Canyon de Chelly, twenty-seven oxen had already succumbed to the steely bite of the cold. In a pincer move from the eastern and western ends of the canyon, columns advanced. They burned hogans, shot livestock, destroyed cornfields and gardens, filled springs with rocks and dirt.

Already in October, the Diné had noticed a flurry of preparations at Fort Canby and started to haul firewood and supplies to the top of Fortress Rock. Initially, some potholes held enough water for the three hundred people holed up on top of the rock. Warriors still made relays to the camps for fresh provisions when their foes were watering horses near the mouth of the canyon at Chinle Wash.

Poles and ladders leading across gaps and up cracks to the top of the fortress were iced up and slippery. Fortress Rock took its toll; people slipped and tumbled like rag dolls into the abyss. As soon as the bluecoats broke camp at the junction of Black Rock and del Muerto canyons, Navajo warriors took up positions behind stone breastworks on the lower ledges. They were ready to defend their families, their lands, their traditions.

At some point, units fired at the citadel from the opposite rim, but found they were too far away to do damage; however, no major battle was waged in the course of this campaign. Many bands had dispersed, pressed by rumors of war. Family groups lived in hiding, as far away as the San Francisco Peaks near Flagstaff, Navajo Mountain, and even the South Rim of Grand Canyon.

Nevertheless, by February exhausted Navajo leaders and their followers began to trickle into Fort Canby. As the season progressed, the trickle turned into a rivulet. The rivulet turned into a stream of hopelessness and defeat. The scorched-earth policy, a merciless winter, and two previous years of drought forced most Diné to surrender.

It almost seemed as if the land itself had turned against them.

During mop-up operations in the canyon, Fortress Rock was briefly besieged, in an attempt to starve out its defenders. When they ran out of water, some warriors courageously climbed down smooth cliffs. They lowered jugs attached to yucca fiber ropes, drawing water from a pool at the foot of the buttress, next to the sleeping soldiers. Eventually, the troops withdrew to Chinle, certain that—if not growling bellies—time itself would bring the refugees to their knees.

## SPIDER ROCK—CANYON DE CHELLY

The sacred counterpart to Navajo Fortress is Spider Rock. Where Canyon de Chelly and Monument Canyon merge, a two-pronged pinnacle of sandstone soars eight hundred vertical feet to the level of both rims. Tsé Na'ashjé'ii (literally, It-Spreads-Something-Sticky Rock) forms the central node in a net of sacred sites that links these canyons, imbuing them with special power. Every spring, medicine men come here to pray and leave feathered prayer sticks, or *kethans*. In this way, *hózhóní*—harmony in the universe—is maintained or restored. The tangle of myths growing around this impressive tower forms but a single strand in the fabric of historical narratives and creation stories that pattern Diné spiritual life and identity.

Spider Woman, one of the most revered characters in Diné as well as Hopi mythology, is said to dwell on the top. She was the first living being in the universe and molded people from the red clay of the earth. To each, she attached a silken thread connected to her, which made palpable the intricacies of existence binding all animated things in mutual obligation and respect. She also instructed the Diné in the weaving of blankets that mimic the hues of this land and have become famous beyond the Colorado Plateau. The first loom consisted of sky and earth cords, a warp stick of sun rays and heddles of rock crystal and sheet lightning. Its batten was carved from a sun halo, the comb from white shell.

A different interpretation of history ascribes the acquisition of weaving to cultural borrowing from Pueblo Indian neighbors. Between the demise of the Ancestral Puebloan civilization before 1300 A.D. and the year-round residency of many Navajo in Canyon de Chelly after 1750 A.D., Hopi families from the mesas to the west seasonally farmed and lived in these canyons. Contact with the Pueblos of the upper Rio Grande valley had also been peaceful until then, offering the Diné opportunities to absorb new techniques and ideas from more sedentary agricultural societies.

Traits that were adopted and modified by the highly adaptive Athabaskan newcomers included a convoluted clan system; methods of gardening and irrigation; peach orchards; and possibly even religious concepts, down to the specific iconography of their rock inscriptions and sand paintings used in healing sessions. A close kinship exists between Pueblo *katsinam*—supernatural beings personified by ceremonial dancers—and masked Navajo Ye'ii' figures. These deities still participate in the great wintertime curing ceremonies, of which the Ye'ii Bicheii is the most prominent.

According to some traditions, Spider Rock and Face Rock, a similar monolith across the canyon, are petrified Holy Beings. They communicate with each other, as echos bouncing back and forth between walls would. The fact that Spider Rock could hardly have been climbed with the equipment Diné warriors had at their disposal is not the reason it never became a rock fortress. People simply believe it is taboo to climb on top of an altar.

FORT DEFIANCE

A lithograph of the fort dated 1856 depicts an idyllic scene. At the mouth of a forested canyon, flat-roofed adobe buildings are neatly aligned around square parade grounds. Mounted horsemen contemplate the setting. Laundry is drying on clotheslines. The Stars and Stripes flaps complacently on the central flagpole, and two ravens soar above everything.

The canyon was long known as Cañoncito Bonito, or Pretty Little Canyon, the plains onto which it opened as Tsehootsoohí, or Meadow-in-the-Rocks. Diné healers convened there to gather herbs used as horse medicine. They threw white shells and pieces of turquoise into springs that bubbled from the rock fold, as payment or pleas for further blessings.

To troops stationed there, Fort Defiance was known as Hell's Gate. They considered it the worst of any frontier assignments: a desolate outpost surrounded by hostile Indians. To thousands of men, women, and children who were rounded up to march into exile and an uncertain future, it would truly become the portal to hellish times.

Colonel Edwin Vose Sumner, who headed one of the first U.S. expeditions into Navajo territory in 1851, quickly realized the strategic potential of the site. It only lay one day's march from the enemies' summer pastures in the Tunichas and Chuskas, and their canyon redoubts. Construction of a post began in September of the same year, and it became the base of operations during subsequent sorties. Defiance truly turned out to be the hoped-for "dagger in the side of the Navajo."

After an uneasy truce with the new rulers, hostilities flared up again in 1856. During a horse race with U.S. soldiers, Diné braves accused their opponents of cheating by tripping one of their mounts. In the ensuing argument and melee, thirty warriors were killed. Four years later, a massive force of one thousand led by the headmen Manuelito and Barboncito attacked the fort that was manned by one hundred fifty infantrymen. The garrison fended off the charge. But, contrary to Western movie clichés, this episode constitutes one of the few documented assaults on a military settlement by Native Americans. Navajo and Apache warriors were even more adept at avoiding pitched battles than their brethren on the northern Great Plains. They had learned to vanish like mirages in the torn, waterless wastes that swallowed pursuers and their mounts.

Fort Defiance was temporarily abandoned and fell into disrepair after 1861, when troops were shifted east in expectation of secession and civil war. In 1863 the largely ruined frontier garrison was restored under the command of Colonel Carson. It was re-christened Fort Canby, after the man who first conceived of the plan to relocate and assimilate the entire Navajo tribe. The removal would finally allow full economic development of territories cleared of intractable, unreliable nomads.

Many fugitives were lured from their holdouts by promises of free food. When they came to the fort for rations, they quickly realized their mistake. While the rounding-up was still in progress, the first prisoners left Canby in February 1864. The first of six major convoys commenced what has become collectively known as the Long Walk. The prisoners were heavily guarded and on foot, in tattered clothes, low on provisions and spirit. Fort Sumner, at the Bosque Redondo in east-central New Mexico, was the destination of a grueling trek that took the Diné more than three hundred miles from their homelands. To this day, that first reservation haunts people as Hwééldí, a Diné pronunciation of *fuerte*, Spanish for "fort."

The largest contingent left the Arizona garrison in March. A seven-mile-long column of soldiers, wagons, and twenty-six hundred Navajo wound its way east. It soon foundered in ten inches of snow. Mount Taylor was the last familiar landmark of which they lost sight, left behind with at least two hundred who died en route. Between 1863 and 1866 more than ten thousand Diné were marched to the banks of the Rio Pecos; approximately three thousand perished, deserted, or were captured by slavers. Diné oral tradition recounts the old, sick, or weak—even pregnant women—who could not keep up and were shot and left unburied, half-naked in the snow.

The location of the new reservation on the lawless fringe of the Llano Estacado had been chosen so that the Navajo would form a buffer against Comanche, who were launching raids from the inaccessibility of the Staked Plains. The bosque had long served as a trade rendezvous. At the same time, it was infamous as a staging area for Apache and Kiowa forays into Old Mexico. Routes for settlers crossing these featureless wastelands had to be marked with stakes, but just as often, skeletons of wagons and horses—or worse—pointed the way.

Nearly nine thousand nomadic Diné at a time were forced to survive on forty square miles, next to Mescalero Apache, who had been confined there already in 1863. Attempts to convert Navajo into "civilized" sedentary pueblo dwellers were soon abandoned. They were allowed to build the customary forked-stick hogans instead, and to live in loose family clusters. Mandatory education failed equally. When soldiers came to take Navajo children to attend school, parents frequently hid them, demonstrating the resilience of a defeated people.

They still had to dig irrigation ditches and till the alkaline soil. Crowded conditions provided a breeding ground for diseases. Mumps, smallpox, and syphilis ruined faces and lives. Mosquitoes hatched in the stagnant water of irrigation canals, spreading malaria throughout the compound. Pneumonia and dysentery plagued the malnourished population. The former was abetted by rags that had to do for clothing, the latter by poor sanitation and brackish water. The twenty-mile-long cottonwood grove that gave the valley its name had soon been cut down for firewood and construction materials. Mesquite had to be dug up laboriously, to keep campfires and inmates alive.

Crops of corn and wheat planted in poor soil failed every single year, devoured by insects and storms. When the numbers at Bosque Redondo exceeded those that could be fed even at half-rations, the post commander at Fort Wingate—a relay station east of present-day Gallup—was ordered not to forward any more prisoners. Army officials had grossly underestimated total numbers of the tribe. Stories have been passed on about Diné boys who picked undigested grain from the manure of well-fed cavalry horses. They roasted and ate it for sustenance. Another oral account tells of rats that were killed. Their meat was chopped up, together with bones and intestines, and shared by up to a dozen people. The Diné also were unfamiliar with many of the foods issued on ration days. Sometimes they just boiled the flour or bacon, or even the green beans of coffee, which they mistook for regular beans. On top of it all, marauding Kiowa and Comanche war parties preyed on the starving Diné, intercepting supplies meant for their relief.

The social fabric as well was severely disrupted. Prostitution (as a means of survival) and witchcraft flourished. Killings of heavily acculturated members of the tribe who had aided the military were typical of the Fearing Time. Conflicts over stolen food escalated between Navajo and the Mescalero Apache, who bolted in 1865 for southern New Mexico and west Texas. From 1866 on, the reservation population dwindled further. More and more Diné drifted back to their old country, where many relatives were still scraping by in secrecy.

Washington was more than unhappy with the costs incurred in support of an experiment that failed to become self-sufficient. Accusations of mismanaged funds and a more humanitarian stance toward American Indians in the wake of the Civil War led to a change of guards. In place of the army, the Quaker-influenced Office of Indian Affairs became responsible for the well-being of the federal wards.

A commission eventually decided that the Diné were better off in their old environment than at Fort Sumner. On June 1, 1868 a treaty was ratified between the government and twenty-seven Navajo headmen, each of whom pledged peace by putting an X on a paper. Its black marks had first been translated into Spanish and from that language into their own. The exiles had toiled four years on foreign soil, before their captors finally allowed them to return to the ancestral lands, to a greatly reduced reservation.

Before their departure, however, the U.S. Army was to impress the Navajo with a demonstration of what would happen if they ever picked up arms again. Soldiers tied a big billy goat to a wooden post in the parade grounds. They hit it repeatedly in the midsection with a stick, so that he butted the post with his head and horns. After a while, his skull cracked, and the brains started leaking out.

So it is told, to this day.

After 1868, Fort Defiance functioned as the Navajo Agency headquarters. Upon their return, each man, woman, and child was given two sheep to start new flocks. Plows, hoes, axes, some old wagons, and annuities for two years as specified in the treaty, were issued with the livestock.

I am searching for remnants of the old garrison at the mouth of Cañoncito Bonito. Indian Social and Health Services now occupy the flats. The facilities include a hospital and a jail. No traces of the original buildings seem to remain, but the streets are still aligned in a military grid. Log cabins and the blank faces of clapboard and natural stone houses line quiet alleys shaded by cottonwoods. No greater contrast to the solitary roundness of hogans and sheep corrals could be envisioned. Between here and Spider Rock lie not just miles, but entire worlds.

Cañoncito Bonito is not so pretty anymore. It now serves as the town dump, and I cannot pick up the babble of its springs. The location of the old post strikes me as rather precarious: the curves of the canyon would cover an enemy's approach to within shooting range. A dirt road slips between sandstone walls. One of the last buildings nestled near the entrance flies the Stars and Stripes on a pole. Unlike in the lithograph, Old Glory looks frayed; the desert sun has bleached its colors. There is no marker or memorial plaque anywhere. No reminder of blood or tears, no reminder of a nation's Manifest Destiny.

A different story is remembered instead. Today is Thanksgiving and, ironically, many Diné celebrate the survival of English pilgrims who landed on Plymouth Rock almost four hundred years ago. In a backyard, a middle-aged Navajo with a buzz-cut takes pity on the wandering stranger who seems lost. He vanishes into the house, only to return with a beer, some canned meat, and half a loaf of sliced bread. He hands everything to me across the fence. "The turkey is still baking," he apologizes with a shrug of shoulders. When I ask questions about the old fort, he admits that he just came over from Gallup to visit for the weekend. No, he does not know anything about the old days.

I sit on a low stone wall. Sipping beer and munching pumpkin pie I bought at a gas station, I still try to tune into this place. I want to be moved by its history. Disappointment descends upon me like a black curtain. What was I really expecting? Picturesque adobe ruins, covered with creeping ivy? Neatly stacked cannonballs next to a bronze statue of a battered, but noble warrior? Another Fort Laramie? Perhaps this is preferable to the romanticizing of a past that never was. Perhaps even the Diné do not want to remember. Perhaps especially not they.

## WHITE HOUSE RUIN—CANYON DE CHELLY

In 1931, with consent of the tribe, President Hoover declared both canyon branches one national monument. Shortly after, a trail used to drive sheep in and out of Canyon de Chelly was widened and smoothed to accommodate tourists. More sightseers began to roll in. They tried to satisfy a re-awakened curiosity in the arts and crafts of Native American cultures. Spectacular ruins and rock art attracted them. So did the prospect to purchase a piece of the Southwest's colorful past.

At present, close to 750,000 people visit each year. The National Park Service administers the sites, but the Navajo Nation still owns the land. To protect the privacy of Diné who still live in the gorges, as well as archaeological treasures, visitors have to be accompanied into the canyons by a park ranger, or a certified Navajo guide.

Tsé Ghá' íldoní, or Blasted-through-Rock, is the only trail that can be hiked without escort. It is also an excellent example for the viability of place-naming traditions reaching back to the Pleistocene.

From the canyon overlook, the path jumps immediately below the rim. It threads a tunnel dynamited through massive rock. The sinuous flow of Permian de Chelly Sandstone speaks volumes about its wind-borne origin. Its lilting layers defy attempts to capture their essence, quickly delineating the limits of poetry or prose or even photography. Slick—in many places overhung—cliffs and cross-bedded fossil dunes glow with the warmth of peaches. They stir the desire to just stand and stare, or even more so, to reach out and touch. Gleaming banners of desert varnish unfurl down slickrock facades. Sturdy Shinarump conglomerate retards lateral erosion atop walls that vary in height from 30 (near the mouth) to 825 (at Spider Rock) feet. This cap of resistant rimrock in combination with the homogeneity of the underlying sedimentary body lends these incisions their steep, narrow, and solid demeanor.

The canyon's name (sounding like "de-shay") does not derive from a corruption of the Spanish or French word for "peach tree" ("pêcher")—alluding to the Navajo peach orchards—as is sometimes assumed. It is rather derivative of *tséyí* ("canyon"), which the Spanish pronounced "chelly" and mistook for a specific name rather than a generic term.

A second tunnel toward the bottom opens upon a pastoral of contemporary Navajo life. A cottonwood, resplendent with golden finery, shades mud-chinked, peeled logs and the green tar-paper roof of a hexagonal *hooghan*, the Diné "home." The beams of this specimen are dovetailed. A central pipe from a fat-bellied cast-iron stove or converted fifty-gallon oil drum pokes through the roof. I know that sleeping platforms inside the single room of this organic structure are arranged against the walls. Most likely, they are covered with sheepskins. Domes of red earth still crown many similar domiciles, which blend perfectly into their surroundings.

Like the saguaro cactus for the Sonoran desert, these rustic Navajo dwellings have become symbols of the Four Corners of the Colorado Plateau. Similar to anthills, their entrances face east, to welcome the new sun and its blessing and warmth on a brisk winter day. Although this particular type of hogan only evolved after the Bosque Redondo period, it contains cosmological references preserved from hunter-gatherer times. Individual architectural elements, but also the structure in its entirety, are representative of the Diné universe.

Mike Mitchell, a medicine man, emphasizes the building's spiritual dimensions: "The hogan has songs and prayers. For a happy dwelling, corn pollen from white corn is placed on the main poles and around the inside in a clockwise direction. From the hogan the Navajos talk, pray, and sing their respect for the mountains, canyons, streams, plants, animals, and everything else that exists."

Where the world is home, the home becomes world.

In a holding pen tucked against the perpendicular cliff, sheep and some billy goats armed with corkscrew horns stand around or lie down, looking bored in the way only grazers can. The clanging of bells and a sharp scent spice the air. Shaggy Angoras were traditionally mixed in with the sheep, because they are better climbers, smarter, and make flocks easier to herd.

Between forty and fifty families still reside in the canyons, mostly during spring planting and fall harvest. Their seasonal round has almost been reversed. People now spend the winter in isolated homesteads on the plateau, or in towns like Chinle, instead of the sheltering hollows below the rim.

Yet another tunnel—this one canopied with Russian olive and tamarisk—leads to the ruins. The warbling of song sparrows leaks through the green screen overhead. The park service planted cottonwood trees and Russian olive bushes after the thirties; they provide shade, and control arroyo cutting, which has done considerable damage to archaeological sites lying at creek level.

A primitive footbridge crosses the streamlet. Ice has begun to sheet the dark water in a jigsaw puzzle of crystals. It crackles and tinkles, awakened by a still vigorous sun.

The ruins of the largest cliff dwelling in the area are indeed impressive. It is estimated that the ancient apartment complex contained as many as eighty rooms and several kivas, split between two levels. About half of the blocky structures cling to the base of the cliff, while the rest perch in an alcove. Tree ladders formerly connected both divisions.

Fences around the perimeter are supposed to protect the site from vandalism. But somebody has beaten the park service to it: bullet holes riddle the pictograph of a crane. And even without binoculars, I can make out an inscription on the gypsum-washed wall of the central building in the shelter that gave the ruin its name. It reads "J. W. Conway. Santa Fe. 1873."

Many consider Kinií Na' ígai (There-Is-a-White-Strip-across-the-Middle-House) the second most sacred place in these canyons, surpassed in holiness only by Spider Rock. It is home to some Holy Beings, including Talking God, who was brought to life by Changing Woman on her way to the Pacific Ocean. Coyote stole part of sleep and gave it to Talking God to safeguard at White House. This is where people's nightmares originate.

A number of chantways are linked with this place, a filigree of esoteric healing-song cycles that appears Byzantine to the uninitiated. Knowledge that sustains or destroys is encoded in them. A power that can work evil or good also inhabits these buildings. It is not tampered with lightly. No Navajo other than a medicine man, a witch, or a fool, will enter this or any of the other ruins, which is one of the reasons for their excellent state of preservation.

Several Diné women have set up folding tables displaying hand-crafted silver-and-turquoise rings, necklaces, bolo ties, and bracelets. Wrist guards and belt buckles with burnished surfaces shimmer like spring water. There are more sellers than buyers this late in the year. While I am scribbling in my notebook, I am reminded that time has not stood still in this place. One of the ladies receives a call on her cell phone. She answers in the mellifluous language of her nomadic ancestors, ancestors who had dozens of words for game animals and hunting implements; for spirits and kin; for plants and rock formations, ceremonies and medicines. But none for trucks, tourists, or fax machines.

English loanwords or newly minted expressions that can be poetic in their straightforwardness weave through contemporary Diné speech. They are proof for the ingenuity and vitality of a culture in flux. I have observed Navajo teenagers whiling away a lazy Sunday afternoon, teeing off from a bluff, in the middle of nowhere. Only sheep were watching the game, their eyes liquid, but without comprehension. I have even listened to talk about a Diné rapper from Albuquerque, who re-traced the Long Walk on foot.

But the People have not always been wise in their choices.

A young Navajo mother once gave me a lift back to the blacktops of civilization. She was snorting coke from her driver's license, with her two-year-old daughter watching silently from the backseat. The child's eyes had held the same expression as those of the sheep at the tee-off.

Back at the overlook, I skirt the rim to get a good look at Meat Rock. This promontory with the marbled finish of a slab of beef possibly also served as a fortress during the Fearing Time. Shards of glass from smashed liquor bottles glitter prettily on the canyon's shoulder. They could be bits and pieces of warriors' pride, of turquoise-decked women's longing for dignity. They could be dreams of a homeland beyond the land-grabbing reach of strangers.

5

# FISH IN A DRY PLACE

*"The unregulated Colorado was a son of a bitch. It was either in flood or in trickle. It wasn't any good."*

—Floyd Dominy, former commissioner
of the Bureau of Reclamation

WHEN I STEP UP TO THE FIRST GOOD-SIZED POOL, SWARMS of small, green-backed fish nervously dart about. These fingerlings cannot be more than one or two inches in length. They zigzag away from my shadow. They hide underneath rocks. They crowd where the pool is deepest, lulled by a false sense of security. Once I crouch down and freeze, they quickly resume their routine of nibbling on neon-green algae, of gulping little insects from the surface.

I have hiked into this hideaway in southeastern Utah to pay my respects to the scaly residents after which it was named—Fish Creek. In the intermittent desert streamlet, remnant populations of suckers, dace, topminnows, and chubs hold out against drought, hikers and cows. From desert springs and isolated tributaries, some western fish that occur nowhere else have branched into scores of sub-species. Many of these now occupy closely circumscribed areas and precarious niches. Genetic isolation is typical of arid environments and makes small populations extremely vulnerable to change. Population biologists still struggle to determine minimal numbers at which these exiled tribes can sustain themselves.

Most desert fish are certainly not very impressive and therefore unattractive to anglers. But the feeling is probably mutual. They nevertheless are unique pieces of the mosaic that evolved in this stingy environment, and as such of scientific and even intrinsic value.

If you are an endangered fish, the Colorado Plateau is not a good place to live. The region has a tradition of piscine abuse that continues to this very day.

Two dams at opposite ends of the state plug major waterways, feed otherwise barren fields and energy-hungry cities, and cause aneurysms in the circulatory system of the Colorado Plateau: Flaming Gorge Reservoir on the Green River, near the Wyoming state line; and Glen Canyon Reservoir in Arizona, better known as "Lake" Powell. The latter bloats nearly two hundred miles of the—once sinuous—Colorado River as it traverses Utah. Sediments necessary for the rejuvenation of beaches are trapped behind the turbine-studded concrete-and-steel arcs, which considerably alter the riparian ecosystem below the dams. Water drained from the depths of these unnatural sinks is, compared to the surface layers or untamed flows, rather chilly.

It causes additional headaches. For many endemic fish species the dance of procreation is fine-tuned to the late spring snowmelt that releases runoff from the mountain ranges of Colorado and Wyoming. After spawning, hatchlings mature in quiet eddies, and tepid backwaters left by the subsiding waters of late summer and fall. But thanks to the Bureau of Reclamation, the bounty of spring is now diverted. It flushes ten million toilets in Los Angeles. It powers air conditioners in Phoenix. It greens golf courses in Las Vegas. The Bureau of Reclamation's monuments to human ingeniousness altered entire aquatic ecosystems, barring some inhabitants from following the primeval call to spawning beds upstream. They changed the distribution and availability of river habitat and food, as well as chemical content and temperature of the water.

Four kinds of native fish unable to tolerate frigid temperatures and other side effects of the dams ended up on the endangered species list: the humpback chub (*Gila cypha*), the bonytail chub (*Gila elegans*), the razorback sucker (*Xyrauchen texanus*), and the carnivorous Colorado pikeminnow (*Ptychocheilus lucius*), formerly known as Colorado "squawfish." The latter—largest member of the minnow family—grows to a streamlined six feet and can weigh one hundred pounds. Historically, it inhabited the entire Colorado River drainage up to its headwaters. It constituted an important food source for settlers and Native Americans in New Mexico, and was harvested commercially in Arizona until 1910. But as their names indicate, most of these fin bearers are neither good eating nor pretty. Nor are they big enough to show off as trophies. Game fish like pike, walleye, sunfish, trout, and bass were therefore introduced by water-managing agencies, and at present nine out of ten fishes in the entire drainage are recent arrivals.

In a matchless display of incompetence and irresponsibility, fishery managers from Wyoming and Utah poisoned more than four hundred miles of the Green River in 1962 with Rotenone. Their goal was to wipe out the "undesirables" supposedly competing with rainbow trout about to be released into the new reservoir at Flaming Gorge. In reality, the predatory trout seriously decimate the fry of desert fish species. The Green and at present still undammed Yampa River of the upper Colorado basin are key reserves for the four species that were already teetering on the brink of extinction. Further havoc was wrought on their numbers when the lethal tide got out of control. It drifted downstream, into the protected waters of Dinosaur National Monument, causing a public uproar. In the end, the chemical warfare unleashed by bureaucrats did not even ensure the survival of record trout. They had to be replaced with two other species of Salmonidae that thrive in clear, fast-flowing water and fared slightly better.

Environmentalists now call for the uncorking of rivers. They are mostly offered a compromise: periodical releases that mimic natural conditions more closely. An experimental flooding of the Grand Canyon in 1996 yielded amazing results. Numerous backwater channels were flushed with fresh nutrients. More important, total beach surface increased by one third. This was indeed a first step to restore native fish nurseries; but it still leaves the problem of water pollution from recreational boating and the tailings piles of abandoned uranium mines. Statistics of the Glen Canyon Institute show that every four years the amount of petroleum products that outboard motors and leaky oil tanks discharge into this "National Sacrifice Area" equals the volume of the *Exxon Valdez* oil spill.

Neither does artificial flooding correct sediment retention by dams. Five tons of sediment accumulate every second behind Glen Canyon Dam alone. According to some estimates, "Floyd's Void" will be rendered obsolete within the next one hundred fifty years. To the delight of a few tourists, siltation will eventually fill the reservoir, turning the dam into a spectacular waterfall.

But more than half of the native fish population in Grand Canyon has already been destroyed. The temperature of water released from well below the reservoir's surface causes additional problems for species like the razorback sucker, which has a narrow temperature window for spawning: from fifty to sixty-five degrees Fahrenheit. The dams by themselves may have had adverse effects. They block spring migrations of pike-minnows that used to travel upstream to reach spawning sites, in imitation of the annual death march of salmon. We should be ashamed of standing by, watching this fish go belly-up, especially before we fully came to understand its story.

This month a major spectacle takes place at Ed Abbey's nemesis, "Lake Foul." It is an endorsement of mass tourism in a place already trampled by more than three million people per year who, in the words of Richard Shelton, prefer illusions, "because they have more than enough reality at home." The reservoir provides the illusion of human mastery and manipulation of nature. It provides the illusion of a carefree lifestyle, of fun without consequences.

Twenty striped bass will be tagged and released into the watery arena. The contestant catching the fish tagged with the grand prize will win $1 million, payable in twenty-five annual installments, without interest. Lesser prizes for other tagged targets include a five-day houseboat vacation on "America's natural playground," a trip to Alaska for two, and a Lake Tahoe vacation package for four. The prizes as well as the event itself are a bizarre mix of "outdoors recreation" and technology promotion. They imply that clouds and rocks and desert wildlife by themselves may not be entertaining enough.

Thus, the Lake Tahoe "package" includes four days in a resort. A dinner/dance cruise on an original paddle wheeler. A half-day sport fishing charter. The one-day rental of a powerboat, or a snowmobile tour. It includes lift tickets, as well as equipment rental to ski "Heavenly," America's largest ski area. (I wonder what they called it before swarms of brightly clad tourists descended upon it.) A final bonus of $100 is the gift certificate for meals and shopping at the resort. Superlatives abound in this kind of poorly disguised advertising, and the fierce pace of organized fun never slows down. So get your tackle boxes and bait, and join the lonely crowd!

Photographic maps titled "Magnificent Lake Powell" are sold to the contestants at every marina. They show the bays and inlets of submerged tributary canyons, rated according to three criteria: fishing, camping, and water-skiing. Pregnant women have been advised not to, but for anglers who actually consider eating their polluted catch, "tasty striper recipes" can be accessed online at www.milliondollarfish.com. I daresay the drab fingerlings in Fish Creek do not envy their flashy tagged-and-released-and-caught-again cousins their brief moments as the focus of cameras.

I imagine what Alaskan elders, with whom I lived and worked north of the Arctic Circle, would have to say about this aquatic "*Wheel of Fortune.*" To them, fishing is communion and part of survival. It is not pastime or sport. Catch-and-release is considered disrespectful toward the spirit of the fish, which offers itself willingly, so that the hunter and his family may live. In southeast Alaska, the homecoming of the first salmon of the year is occasion for a major religious festival of thanksgiving and remembering. Fish bones are returned to the streams, so that salmon may reincarnate. These practices and beliefs may sound quaint to city slickers, but even in our culture we berate children for playing with, or wasting, their food.

Championing the stressed fish, I cheered upon hearing that this year at Glen Canyon the Big One got away.

Everybody has fishing stories.

On my way into a side canyon of the reservoir, I was once invited by two friendly boaters to go on a fishing trip. They said they could drop me off at the mouth of my canyon, which would spare me the walk in from the highway. Since I was also curious about the "houseboat mentality," I agreed to come along.

The boat's owner was a Mormon Good Ole Boy from Salt Lake City. His pride was the "fish-finder," a device that looked as if it could have been salvaged from a nuclear submarine. If not outnumbered, the fish were clearly outgunned. Fluorescent green dots on the monitor betrayed not only numbers and approximate sizes, but also the depth at which our prey was hanging out.

We still did not catch any fish. At least while I was on board. What do you do then, on a fishing trip where you don't drink booze or catch fish? You talk outboard motors and religion. You hope that your destination is close. I have been on many hunting and fishing excursions, but never—before or since—on one where beer and coffee and tall-tales were not staples.

Leaving the fish refuge behind, I amble down-canyon, reminded that the blessings of surface water in dry places are a mixed lot indeed. Deerflies are attacking viciously, always going for the back of my legs, as if they were trained to target this most vulnerable place. I cut a switch off some rabbitbrush and whip myself down the trail like a medieval penitent. I finally realize that horses were given tails for a reason.

I lunch high above the canyon floor, in an airy alcove harboring Anasazi ruins. Beyond the tips of my boots, more than six hundred feet below, I can make out brambles of wild roses. I look down upon the violet-green backs of swallows wheeling and flashing white rump spots.

While I munch stale crackers and cheese, I replay in my head conversations about the river that lies broken behind Glen Canyon Dam. One of my good friends concedes beneficial influences even to something as denatured as the reservoir. He is convinced that any exposure whatsoever to the great mystery of nature will eventually lead to respect. This respect in turn will foster a desire to protect wilderness and diversity. I, on the other hand, am pessimistic to the point of misanthropy. I usually taunt him with a study of zoo visitors and whale watchers conducted by some evolutionary psychologists, who put to test E. O. Wilson's "biophilia hypothesis."

According to Wilson, the human species evolved as an integral part of a specific natural environment, and a tendency to focus on its workings and our fellow creatures bestowed a selective advantage upon us. The affiliation with wild life forms and natural processes is not just a preference, but simply a biological need. Its suppression, which is typical of modern life in the industrialized world, comes at the price of neurosis and alienation. To complicate matters further, this innate "obsession" with nature can manifest itself in fear and destructive behavior as well.

The results of the research were discouraging. They showed that zoo visits are foremost an occasion to be with family. Experiencing the animals is often considered to be of secondary importance. Furthermore, the impact is transient and superficial, no real learning occurs. If anything, people feel reassured of their perceived birthrights as the crown jewels of creation. Summarizing the results, Stephen Kellert comments "the typical visitor appears only marginally more appreciative, better informed or engaged in the natural world following the experience."

On a busy weekend, Lake Powell can indeed turn into a zoo. Except that here, the monkeys are loose. I have a gut feeling that this research is equally valid in both settings. Both experiences are largely non-participatory; the spectators are isolated from nature's messiness, either by iron bars and fences, or by boat hulls of plastic and steel. Ensconced in protective shells, they are surrounded by a second defense line—that of engine noise. In the case of zoos, wildlife has been taken out of context; postmodern pastiche has replaced authentic, lived-in environments. In the "Lake" Powell scenario, nature has been engineered to fit human purposes. Place has been degraded into mere scenery, wildlife into ornaments.

I descend from my lofty roost. A fierce wind has sprung up, lashing the surface of pools to white frenzy. Zephyr's blasting keeps the deerflies at home. It also raises clouds of dust from the slopes, depositing red silt in my ears, eyes, and nostrils. Forget about character-building hardship! I grind my teeth and decide on the spot to buy a fishing rod and head down to the beachheads. An air-conditioned vacation on a sanitized lake in California is just what I need.

6

# DEATH HOLLOW

*"If there is magic on this planet, it is contained in water."*

—Loren Eiseley, anthropologist

I MAGINE A BEND IN THE CANYON. WHERE THE STREAM RUBS against monolithic sandstone foundations, it has dug out an alcove. The niche is not quite large enough to hold a single-room cabin. Tresses of maidenhair fern trail from rock fissures, netting water droplets like tiny silver fish. A single box elder crowns a slab fallen from the ceiling; its branches droop, as if reaching for the aquamarine pool at its foot. In a dance of gold filigree, reflections ripple across the ceiling's half-shell. Sand finer than sugar coats the bottom of pool and alcove alike, an unblemished beach straight out of Sindbad's tales. Swallows dart in and out of the shelter. They rise, dive, and coast. They spin on the tips of their wings, as if on invisible hinges.

I recline in the pool. Up to my lower lip in clear water, I savor long drafts of it. Dragonflies alight on boulders and—apparently unconcerned—on the twin-islands of my knobby knees, which poke from the surface. Their bodies are slivers of coral and sky, their wings as insubstantial as baby breath, or frost on a windowpane. When I hold still, warbling from the bushes blends with the cadence of water. The time is now, the place—Death Hollow.

I climbed into its stone innards the previous evening. Daylight had long relaxed its hold; only a smear of lavender hesitated above the western horizon. Darkness was replacing depth, erasing more and more details. In the failing light it became hard to negotiate the Moqui steps stitching nearly vertical cliffs like a zipper.

Sadly leaning poles, rock piles, and rusted wire snags indicated the route I had traced across the plateau's corrugation to the canyon. It had once been part of the Boulder Mail Trail, which connected the Utah towns of Escalante and Boulder. Pack mule and telegraph line linked these Mormon outposts to each other, as well as to the outside world. Boulder had been the last community in the United States to have its mail delivered by muleback—three times a week—until 1929. Under much sweating, the townsfolk had chopped footholds from the rock, to provide safe purchase for pack animals. But quite a few mules had met their maker on the way down, and the idyllic place soon earned a reputation.

I had pitched my tent in the gloaming, at the canyon's bottom. I sensed more than saw huge trees straining upward, like columns of a Gothic cathedral. A springy carpet of conifer needles gave with every step and made for sweet dreaming. When dawn bronzed the rim, chattering jays welcomed me to their grove of ponderosa pines. The trees seemed to finger the new light up high. I pressed my three-day stubble against the bark; it was hard to say which was scratchier. Unashamed, I inhaled the familiar fragrance of vanilla.

"Tree hugger" is an epithet hurled at environmentalists who chain themselves to old-growth trees to prevent clear-cutting. But have you ever really hugged a ponderosa? Have you swayed with the tree in a breeze, in an intimate dance? Have you felt the groaning of wood in the pit of your stomach? Self-consciousness, or the fear of looking ludicrous is what *truly* separates us from trees.

A number of Native American cultures have embraced these evergreens for their medicinal properties. They burn the spent husks of cones and put the resulting ashes on sores. The tree's blood mixed with bear grease is spread on infections or chapped skin. Ingested as syrup against pneumonia or whooping cough, it opens respiratory passages.

In tribal cultures nourished by oral tradition, the death of an elder is often mourned more than the death of an infant. It is believed that the loss of such a repository of experience, wisdom, and knowledge is the greater tragedy for the group. (It has been compared to the burning-down of a library.) Even in a society that worships youth and growth and potential, this sentiment still influences how many of us regard ancient trees. More than anything, I admire these giants for their roots, for the riches that reside in deep memories of just one place.

I broke camp early that first day. I had hoped to get a good lead before the sun would burst into flames and slow life down almost to a standstill, melting the marrow in my bones. But at some point, the lure of the canyon's natural bathtubs had simply overwhelmed me.

Before my motivation completely dissolves I get out of the water, though very reluctantly. I am not even fully dressed when the heat has already licked my skin dry. As I wend my way downstream, blossoms in the undergrowth compete for attention. The solitary chalices of evening primroses—white before pollination, pink or lavender afterward—still slumber as tender buds. They only unfold late in the afternoon. This biennial hoards all its energy, to flaunt death in one single day of glory.

The spherical heads of showy milkweed are barely able to contain all their pink starbursts. The Paiute, who used the plant's sap as chewing gum, call it Milk Squirter. Caterpillars of the monarch butterfly consume its toxic leaves, adopting a quirky defense strategy. The strange diet makes them unpalatable to predators, and most birds learn their lesson quickly.

Insect life does not want to be bested in this contest of colors: damselflies in the bright hues of the rainbow are visiting potholes. Bluets, the largest genus of this many-branched clan, resemble twigs dipped in electric blue paint; black markings have been dripped along their rumps. Their eye bulges and crystal wings shine like an oil slick in a puddle. Voracious little helicopters, they snatch insects on the wing, with a dexterity that inspired Native American hunters to honor them with the name Mosquito Hawk. Swallowtails the size of my palm tumble near the water's edge, tail-like protrusions sprouting from back wings. Their black tiger-stripes and wing borders set off a veined pattern against the lemon-yellow background. Painted ladies daintily sip from flower heads, batting their wings like eyelashes.

No animal, however, embodies the spirit of place better than a bird. My scientifically inclined self is willing to attribute the presence or absence of particular species to seasons, to migration corridors, predators, availability of nesting material, and food niches. The poetic savage in me wants to believe that a canyon's personality expresses itself in a specific kind of bird. First sightings are never forgotten. In my imagination, Coyote Gulch brought forth the summer tanager, Spring Canyon gave birth to the Virginia's warbler, and Sulphur Creek lives as the water ouzel. In the mirror halls of the mind, the reverse is also true: hundreds of song lines sing as many canyons into existence. Memory is tied to places, and so is creation.

Death Hollow has been reincarnated in avian flashes of sky, clouds, and red rock. It can be glimpsed flitting behind a screen of juniper trees. The head of a male lazuli bunting recalls the baldachin of the desert sky, its chest throbs with the color of surrounding cliffs, and clouds reflect off his snowy belly. In their endless interweaving of human and non-human history, the Paiute believe the harlequin feathers are beadwork on buckskin clothes the bird wore, when it was still quasi-human. Long ago, buntings also spoke the same language as people.

And on a day like this, I feel only a breath away from being able to talk to them once again.

Around lunchtime, I run into a group of Scouts accompanied by their adult leaders. They started at Hell's Backbone, a rough-and-tumble dirt road creasing the shoulder of Boulder Mountain. Their faces are flushed, their packs, T-shirts, and army pants filthy and torn. The ragged bunch is running on nothing but fresh air and the high-octane fuel of exhilaration. Politely, they ask if I have any food to spare. And how far it is to the confluence, from where they will hike out to the highway.

After quick handouts of candy, they forge ahead, ready for burgers, showers, clean socks. I watch them disappear down the trail, hoping this jaunt has left indelible impressions in their young minds. Will they remember? When their time comes to approve of drilling or strip-mining these mesas and canyons, will they remember?

Cauliflower clouds have crept up to the canyon rims all morning, piling on top of each other. Blossoming. Boiling. Nudging. Slowly changing to the dull gray of slate. Now heaven's spillways open, and a typical late-summer deluge thrums on the canopy of cottonwood and box elder leaves. I seek refuge in an undercut, for its framed view and the feeling of shelter it offers, rather than to stay dry. I am already drenched to the skin, from wading and swimming narrows that deepen as they approach the Escalante River.

Before the powdery soil has a chance to turn into muck, the rain stops—as abruptly as it began. The sun instantly converts the canyon into a greenhouse, filling my nostrils with earthy aromas. Moisture drips from dense foliage. Curlicues of steam rise from the ground. Rows of drops cling to box elder branches and dangle from bent reeds. With the slightest aftermath of wind, they quiver and blink in prismatic colors. Entire constellations find room on one leaf.

There are two phenomena the desert buff never tires of watching: flames of a campfire, hollowing out a winter night, and water running against the wilting of summer. Both are more than simply visual pleasures. Both engage smell, skin, hearing, the heart and the mind. In the presence of both, one cannot help but feel the comfort of living creatures.

In these clefts, water embodies more than just an erosive force. I have to remind myself that the riches of Death Hollow were only made possible by the life-giving medium. All desert people remember and honor this intimate connection. One of the Navajo words for water translates as "long body," referring to the shape it often assumes in desert runnels. A prominent Diné healer sums up this element's magical power: "Where water is, there are living things. Where water is, life goes on. In a holy way it flows. It is alive in a holy way."

Pressed to pick his favorite natural subject, a Moab friend chooses fluid dynamics, always and without hesitation. Pete is a mathematician and fellow river guide, which may explain his fascination with the liquid medium to a degree. Both of us are forever enthralled by the behavior of water. Whorls and eddies, vortices and waves form graphs in the fractal geometry of rivers and creeks. Sand dunes and clouds, rock strata, rainsqualls, and even birdsong seem to follow the same equations. Reaching beyond the realm of nature, this geometry links capillary waves to chaos theory. It joins hydraulic bores and Hokusai's print, "The Great Wave off Kanagawa." It weds the deflection of water molecules to the swirling intricacies of Ligeti's music.

An upright stick in the pellucid flow of Death Hollow trembles against the life of the current. On its upstream side, the surface is crimped with tension, taut with the concussion of energy, and the attractive chevron design is mimicked at the sandy bottom, in a hypnotic flutter of light.

Rounding a coil of the chasm, I witness a spectacle even more rare in its transience. Rain sheeting off wrinkled tablelands has been funneled into increasingly deeper grooves. It arcs from a notch in the rim and descends like a curtain in front of an alcove—one hundred, two hundred feet. Mist wafts over the plunge pool. Frenetic applause and foot stomping ring through the hollow.

With ferocity, the water tries to keep me from swimming into the white chamber of madness. Current and spray join to blind me, to push me away from the impact zone. I finally manage to squeeze under the falls, but can hardly breathe in the vaporous turmoil. For seconds that stretch into eons, nothing seems to exist outside of this pounding. Pummeled some more by watery fists, I begin to worry about the possibility of debris shooting down with the flow. When I crawl out to shore, my skin tingles from the rough handling.

Death Hollow has undergone a miraculous transformation: the limpid and playful creek has been infused with sediment. Swollen and flustered, it now shows off its brawn like a barroom brawler.

Less than a mile downstream from the temporary jet, its thunder subsides, eclipsed by the serenity of the Escalante River. The tributary's discharge inscribes muddy scrolls into the olive-green main current, reminders of the commotion up-canyon. Nowadays, the Escalante drains into Glen Canyon Reservoir, contributing its share of silt, and choking it. For each linear mile, the river meanders more than two through this splendid chunk of desert, in no hurry to meet its demise.

The stream is a living monument for two Franciscan friars, Fray Silvestre Vélez de Escalante and Fray Francisco Atanasio Domínguez. They trekked across the uncharted badlands of Utah in 1776, but actually never set foot on this river's crooked banks. Suffering five months of grueling heat and terrain, the expedition covered two thousand miles, in an attempt to link Santa Fe with the Californian missions near Monterey. The main goal was to scout sites for new settlements: presidios and missions would string across pagan country like beads on a rosary. Bedazzled by the hostile topography of one of the harshest environments on the North American continent, the friars and thirteen compadres lost too much time in their wanderings. When winter threatened to overtake them, they decided to head back to New Mexico, mission unaccomplished. Homeward bound, they became the first Europeans to reach the Colorado River where it is shielded on both sides by echoing cliffs. They were facing one more obstacle that almost broke their faith.

An initial attempt to ferry over in crude paddle rafts failed miserably. Wrapped in desperation, they christened a camp at the confluence of the Paria and Colorado Rivers in Marble Canyon San Benito "Salsipuedes"—"get out if you can." Local Paiute informed the explorers of an ancient ford close by, which was part of the Ute War Trail, the only established route through the region dominated by Navajo Mountain. Between 1870 and 1880 Mormons from southern Utah dynamited the rocky approaches to this crossing, to protect their settlements against Diné and Ute horse raiders.

At a place that later became known as The Crossing of the Fathers, the starving party finally managed to wade across, waist-deep in water. A commemorative plaque marking the exact spot where the Colorado was forded now lies flooded, as do steps hacked from cliffs with Spanish steel, and nearby Padre Creek. One of the premier historical sites of the state has been lost to the public.

Had the friars succeeded in pioneering a viable track between New Mexico and California, Hispanic rule would have wielded a strong influence on the territory. It possibly could even have stalled colonization by the Latter-day Saints. Chicano culture and language would prevail in southern Utah, as they do in southern Arizona and New Mexico. The beer would be strong and called cerveza, salsa the music and condiment of choice. And food would only be surpassed in its fire by the passions of señoritas with hair glossy as freshly laid tar.

# 7

# WIND

*"It is only by means of wind that we talk. It exists at the tip of our tongues."*

—Anonymous Navajo singer

THE GALE THAT STAMPEDED DOWN THE GORGE SNORTED and whinnied like a frightened horse. Dust from its beating hooves quickly smothered the stars. With nowhere else to go, it battered the tent, trying to break through the door. I was forced to leave the warm cocoon of my sleeping bag repeatedly, to weigh down the stakes with rocks. For long hours, the flapping tent fly kept me awake.

When I crawl out of my shelter this morning, I feel sapped of all strength. A glaze of sleet encases the nylon like a second skin, but fortunately, no poles were broken.

Last night's storm did not come as a surprise. Perched atop the Waterpocket Fold, near the canyon's brink, I had watched the afternoon grow sullen. As the cloud ceiling crept down the flanks of the Henry Mountains, it seemed to obliterate the world one bite at a time. When I returned to camp, the wash was adrift with sand. Sand piled around the bases of bushes. Sand stung my calves. Sand pelted my pack. It hissed on my tent. Inside, everything had been sifted over with a layer of ruddy dust. It looked as if the desert was claiming ownership of my belongings.

Spending much time in the back-of-beyond, you become attuned to the weather as much as to the geology and topography of a place—because it can be your ally or enemy. Stuck in bottomless hollows, sequestered from the horizons, you are always at risk of being assailed by blizzard, flash flood, or thunderstorm. At the very least, the red squalls can be a bother: on stormy days, the sediment they carry clings to your hair, food, and notebooks. It clogs zippers, camp stoves, and your nostrils, and you wear it like makeup or camouflage. It tints creeks and bushes, your vision, your very soul. It deepens the color of sunsets. Dunes accumulate on the lee side of ridges, slowing down the already weary backpacker. If the blasts catch you off balance, they may even topple you from a skinny ledge. How many times in your life have you had to wrestle an animated tent to the ground?

I once witnessed a desert fall gust pick up a sixteen-foot raft from a trailer, knocking down a river guide in the process. Normally, it takes two people a few minutes to unload such a boat. The wind sent it cartwheeling down the beach like a toy, then—like a bored child—dropped it a hundred feet from shore into the stream.

On a more positive note, bliss in the desert can be as simple as a breeze that caresses your burning face, keeping mosquitoes, deerflies, and heat exertion at bay.

The vocabulary of geographers glitters with terms for artifacts of the wind that were borrowed from Turkish and Arabic languages: s*erir*, *reg*, *barchan*, *yardang*, and *seif*—the latter describing a scimitar-shaped, sharp-crested dune. Beyond merely honing the physique and character of desert dwellers, abrasive, sand-laden winds have been their nemesis forever. Already Herodotus, the

Greek historian, mentioned an unfortunate Tunisian army perishing in the fangs of a *harmattan,* that searing curse of the western Sahara. The cymbal- and drum-beating troops failed to keep its white-hot shriek from advancing. There was no way to prevent the drying-up of waterholes, the dying of men and their mounts.

Mile-high dust clouds, solid as walls, are occasionally unleashed by Sudan's *haboob,* and similar phenomena have been observed in North America's southwestern deserts. The pyramid-burying *khamsin* of Egypt, the *simoom'* or "poison wind" of Arabia, and the *buran* afflicting Central Asian nomads with fever, all share equally bad reputations.

The discipline of medical climatology is still in its infancy. But current research is exploring the possibility of connections between physical reactions in people or animals, and atmospheric disturbances. One study concluded that winds resembling the Chinook increased blood pressure, as well as the incidence of heart attacks and strokes. Asthma and arthritic pain also supposedly worsen under windy conditions. Because body and mind are entwined, it is in the end difficult to clearly separate physical from emotional causes. Undoubtedly, wind induces stress in many people, and such agitation can affect people's ailments. Is it any wonder really, that the Hindu paradise Nirvana is a place "without wind"?

In spite of danger and discomfort, I try not to mind the weather's bluster all that much. If each day were as smooth as a pearl, none would stand out from the rest.

By noon, the last cloud tatters have beaten a hasty retreat, and the sky has been rinsed ultramarine. Last night's ordeal is forgotten. The spirit soars. Between patches of wet ground, woody vines of old man's beard creep over boulders and bushes, using them as crutches, or anchoring them against future storms. The feather tufts of female seeds quiver on puffs of air, as if alive.

❖❖❖❖

People learned to modify their outfits, to cope with the wither-
ing breath of the desert by wearing burnooses and bandannas.
Plants adapted through natural selection, developing a cornu-
copia of strategies. Those that did not became locally extinct. By
reducing surface area as well as changing the shape of their
leaves, Mormon tea, juniper, rabbitbrush, sage, snakeweed, saltbush, tamarisk, and scores of other thrifty greenery managed to
slow down evaporation, which increases in windy climes.
Evergreen trees like the pinyon pine obeyed the same principle,
trading leaves for needles. Precious water is also retained with
the help of a waxy coating that seals off the leaves of manzanita
or barberry bushes. The whip-like stalks of ocotillo only sprout
costly foliage after sufficient rain has fallen. In many desert-
dwelling plants, the breathing pores (or "stomata") necessary
for water and gas exchange have sunk well into the leaf surface,
keeping water from being wicked away by the wind. Tiny pockets of water vapor exhalations remain in the sunken pits above
the little mouths. Precious moisture is often further detained by
fine guard hairs. Succulents like yuccas and agaves have reduced
surfaces in favor of fleshy leaves that store additional water in
internal cells not available for photosynthesis. As plants highly
adapted to arid conditions, they have been able to reduce evaporative transpiration enormously.

The masters of water conservation are, without doubt, cacti.
They dispensed with leaves altogether, storing the chlorophyll
that fuels photosynthesis entirely in their succulent trunks. Their
leaves devolved into spines, barbs, and "glochids," fine bristles
that irritate the lips of eager gourmets. In addition to warding off
browsers, they break up moisture-sucking air currents.

A few plants even take advantage of the atmospheric commotion. Tumbleweed, the icon of Western freedom and desola-

tion, is not native to this region at all. But this stowaway from the steppes of Russia is a perfect match for our windswept ranges, another rags-to-riches immigrant story. As Russian thistle matures, it breaks loose from the overgrazed soil it prefers. The skeleton bushes bounce and roll until caught in ditches and fences. Numberless seeds are thus spread at the speed of a cantering horse. Within only a few decades from its accidental introduction into South Dakota, this transplant had conquered the entire intermountain West.

Evaporative cooling saves backpackers, who sweat profusely under their loads, from overheating. In addition, body heat is whisked away by the wind's buffeting. For many fur-covered desert mammals, nature offered a different solution. Mule deer, kit foxes, and jackrabbits grew oversized, fine-veined ears that help them shed excess metabolic heat. When the sun is snuffed out, cold beds down in the high country; the wind commences its moaning, and rabbits can often be seen with ears folded tightly against their back—shielding the precarious flame.

Wind marks the round dance of seasons in Canyon Country, arousing the senses. At about this time, on mesa tops across the Southwest, the kiss of spring air teases pinyon pines into releasing clouds of pollen gold. Sweet breezes broadcast the aphrodisiacal schemes of blossoming cliff rose, mingled with skeins of cedar incense and the clacking of deer hoof rattles and chanting that plead for rain to come to the crops. The brilliance of hummingbirds, the translucence of monarchs is delivered north with the balm of the surging currents.

When Zephyr arrives, the tails of his mares twitch across robin egg skies. Dust devils spin like dervishes through the desert. Thunderheads and sandstorms muscle their way in on late summer monsoons, while the yearning of coyotes eddies and swirls through the nights.

This is also the season when anabatic (up-slope) and katabatic (down-slope) winds seek a way through red rock mazes. As air warms and expands throughout the day, it soars up-canyon. After sunset, cooling and contracting, it folds its wings and plummets back down, as a result of the differential heating of mountains and canyons.

The tranquility of fall is only occasionally stirred by a gentle touch that disrobes aspen and cottonwood trees. A water ouzel's burbling floats on autumnal flows, promising comfort. Above craggy mountain heads, turkey vultures gather in "kettles." Seething and roiling in thermal vortices, they seek their cruising altitude, finally tapping into rivers of air that will carry them south.

Sighs weave through stunted junipers as the old year expires. They join the bone rattling of bulrushes and yucca stalks and the brittle susurrations of leaf litter in a dirge. Always too soon, winter's breath stuns life in treetops, burrows, and creeks. Its sting drains the land of color. When spindrift finally chases snowflakes into chimneys and cracks, baring branches and slickrock backs, things have come full circle.

The upper part of this drainage is quietly famous among canyon aficionados for its large number of natural arches. It even includes a few double and triple spans, which open like windows along this geological fault. Contrary to the Old Norse origin of "window" (from "wind-eye") and the belief of newcomers to the Colorado Plateau, wind is *not* the major force responsible for sculpting these peepholes into the blue yonder. Two hundred million years of sandblasting have only polished contours, which were planed and whittled by frost and flood, to a delicate finish. The amazing array of arches, fins, spires, and balanced rocks was released from its matrix by desert water.

Ancient winds, however, *did* lend a hand in the deposition of sand and dust freed from its parent rock. Jurassic dune fields gave birth to the ivory borders that now hem in this canyon. During the Mesozoic, nearly indestructible loose quartz crystals became airborne and—eventually dropped by the tiring winds— piled layer upon layer. Under pressure and chemical bonding they fused into the emblematic rock strata of the Southwest. Their resilience is such that some have been through the mill of weathering, erosion, and deposition not just once, but several times. The aeolian origin of Navajo Sandstone is evident in the crossbedding of wafer-thin strata, which laminate knolls and domes. When a dune accumulates, some of its sand will cascade down the steep leeward slope or "slipface." These miniature avalanches form distinct planes that remain after the dune turns to stone. The dips and slants of onionskin layers of rock can also be signs of shifting wind directions, possibly also accounting for slight variations in color.

According to a cliché, mystery can be found in a grain of sand. Even more mystery can be found in *windblown* grains of sand. At high air velocities, sandy surfaces begin to creep. Ripples begin to swim. Entire dunes start to migrate; their normally crisp outlines become a blur. This is not just another heat-induced delusion. Sand grains skip and bounce along the ground like a plague of fleas, in a process known as "saltation." On impact, they crash into other grains, knocking them loose and forward, which accounts for the characteristic hissing. Once in motion, they continue even when the wind slows down. Finer particles remain airborne and travel farther—as dust. Granules too heavy to be moved are left behind.

With each easterly twist of the creek bed, I face the heavy varnish of Navajo Sandstone scarps. They appear as formidable obstacles, more than a thousand feet high, and seemingly without foot- or handholds. But each time, the cornered wash ends up dodging the trap, snaking its way through the fold. Alcoves like flaring band shells undermine canyon walls that now pinch the wash in their vise grip. Where turbulences of long-gone floods dissolved the cement of metal oxides, silica, and calcium carbonate that bound individual sand grains, honeycombed perforations riddle the sandstone. The Diné think of these solution cavities as the work of "whirling spirits," stepladders for the wind. The life force itself is conceptualized as wind; whorls, like cowlicks, fingerprints, or ear folds serve as entryways. *Nilch'i* , or Holy Wind enters a person with a baby's first cry. Part of it is also passed on from both parents. It inflates bodies that otherwise would only be sacks of skin and bone, keeping them upright and centered between heaven and earth. This Wind Soul influences one's thoughts and behavior, determining the course of a life. If advice from "the wind within" is ignored, it weakens and finally dies. And so does its vessel. By means of prayer sticks and healing ceremonies, the winds may be petitioned to restore the vitality of a patient. Upon death it departs. Blowing onward, it eventually lodges in another being, human or non-human.

Superficially resembling the Christian idea of a soul, *nilch'i* is actually closer to the Buddhist concept of *chi*. It endows creatures with thought, with speech, and the power of motion and serves as the means of communication between them and all elements of the living world. External and internal winds are not distinct in this philosophy of nature. Supreme Sacred Wind was the creator of the Diné universe, and still guards the earth. Different winds whisper directly into people's ears, providing guidance. They reside in the cardinal directions and warn of dangers. Amber-eyed owls are their messengers.

Echoing Western medical and psychological research on potentially unwholesome effects of wind, the Diné worldview acknowledges the influence of environmental factors upon human behavior and well-being. On the flip side, people are able to acquire a certain amount of control over forces of nature. They can impose order on the external world by acts of ritual speech: prayer, chant, and storytelling. Long alien to our own ways of thinking, these ideas show a grasp of reality that is now frequently validated by ecology, psychology, and other modern scientific disciplines.

In the complementary and fluid world of the Navajo, each force can also mutate into its opposite. Holy Wind may shift to become "breath poison." Evil powers conjured by witches are inhaled, invading the body through its orifices. They become visible as dust devils, or "cylindrical ghosts," which frequently rotate, "unnaturally," against the direction of the sun's course. These downsized tornadoes are the spirits of those who let their *nilch'i* whither, thereby dying prematurely.

East is the lair of the black wind in the color-coded universe of the Diné. Winds from the east brought land-hungry settlers and their diseases across the Atlantic. They propelled the billowing canvases of Conestoga wagons over vast prairie seas. Easterlies rang with the fanfare blasts of conquistadors and played with the standards of pale-eyed horse soldiers.

Now the dark winds of progress are howling again. The exhalations from the planet's green lungs have become shallow and labored. The self-healing powers of an atmosphere normally flushing its skies clean with snow and rain have been corrupted. A sickly stench from cities and coal-burning plants spreads acidic rain like rumors; smoke from mismanaged forests weakens the sun. "Downwinders," who lived through the cold war, are eaten alive by tumors brought on by nuclear testing, unpredictable winds, and sheer disregard. The desert is advancing on a global front, spearheaded by Dustbowl-specters feeding on overgrazed topsoil. Perhaps the medieval assumption that malaria and plague were brought forth by putrescent mists rising from the earth was metaphor rather than medical theory.

But wind will abide, unbridled. In a post-apocalyptic scenario envisioned by writer and culture critic Edward Abbey, it keens through sagging power lines, etches windows, strips street signs and abandoned cars of their paint, slowly drowns malls and overpasses in sand, turning metastasizing cities into mausoleums. Good News indeed.

In the lower canyon I rest in the largest undercut, surrounded by crumbling cow pies, rusty tin cans, and pack rat tracks crisscrossing the dust. This cowboy camp opens easily two hundred feet deep into the cliff. Buckaroos have used it since the twenties. It probably also sheltered hunters of the Fremont culture, but any signs of earlier occupation have been obliterated by pothunters or cattle.

By the time I finish a meager dinner, the storm has returned with doubled strength. It rushes by the entrance, roaring, kicking, and wailing. Trapped once again. Around dusk, it calms down, exhausted. Temperatures drop, large snowflakes tumble from a livid sky; with barely audible whispers they settle on the ground outside the alcove. I roll out my pad and sleeping bag. And my thoughts begin to drift.

John Atlantic Burr was a rancher who pioneered a stock trail through this canyon. Delivered on board an emigrant vessel, halfway between Scotland and Utah, he was given the middle name of his stormy birthplace. One day, rounding up cattle on this godforsaken range, he tried to relieve a severe urinary tract infection with a piece of baling wire. Huddled under an overhang somewhere nearby, he cursed the desert under his breath. But an indifferent wind scattered the dying man's words.

8

# DOWN THE RIVER WITH
# ED AND THE MAJOR

*"In my boat I carried enough food for two
weeks, a one-man tent, a sleeping bag, some
warm clothes in a rubberized bag, five gallons
of drinking water, and the many other little items
needed for a week or more in the wilds—cigars,
bourbon, the Portable Tolstoy, matches, Demerol
tablets, pen, notebook, a .357 and a P-38."*

—Edward Abbey, part-time river
runner and full-time curmudgeon

THE GROWLING OF MONSTER TRUCKS AND STACCATO OUT-
bursts from a jackhammer biting through concrete rend the
thick air. Workmen in helmets and orange safety vests are balancing on steel girders spanning the stream. The Green River
Bridge is closed to all traffic.

With the help of a friend who drove shuttle from Moab, I
sneak my canoe and gear across the back lawn of the John
Wesley Powell Museum of River History. A quick farewell, and
I slip into the current. Paddling hard, I manage to stay clear of

the pylons. I regret not having time to take in the museum's exhibits, but am eager to get some miles under my keel before darkness settles on the river.

The Denver and Rio Grande Western Railroad Bridge and the interstate pass overhead, then I shrug off town like a shabby coat. Before me stretch one hundred twenty river miles. Miles rich with promise, shrouded in mystery. Good country in which to feel young again, and free.

Two readings are stowed away in a waterproof bag: a sheaf of photocopied pages from Powell's account of his first run down this section of the Green River, and an essay collection by Edward Abbey, dog-eared and water-stained, as if it had been down the river a few times itself. I left the bulk of the Powell volume at home. Planning to hike out through the Needles district of Canyonlands National Park, I gladly consent to carry Abbey's soaring phrases, but not the explorer's hefty prose. Though normally not prone to gushing or hero worship, I have to admit that Abbey's words *did* change my life. That is why I am out here, following in his wake.

At the first oxbow outside of town, two mule deer does browse next to the river. In the crystal clarity of this late November afternoon, every single hair of their coats seems to stand out. If one could cut this light, it would bleed. Cottonwoods line both banks like torches whose glow leaks onto the still waters. A great blue heron stalks in the shallows. Its steps are tentative, as if the bird did not trust the river to bear its weight.

Why did they come? Blank spots on his maps, thirst for knowledge and recognition lured Powell. Abbey saw the rivers and canyons of the Southwest as the last escape from lives "pretty well caged in by the walls, bars, chains and locked gates of our industrial culture." Running rivers is a habit that is hard to give up. Let me be frank and call it an addiction.

In the early eighties, Abbey already complained that western waterways were getting too crowded and vowed to forsake them: "I have had more than my share," he lamented, "and don't intend to do any more." But he quickly changed his tune to "hardly any," and "one more river, one more time." Next thing, he drew up a list of notorious rivers all over the world that he still wanted to run.

I wonder what he would say if he saw the recent snowballing of "adventure tourism." The rivers have transmogrified into water parks. Jet boats carry droves of passengers, plowing the tan waters between Moab and the Confluence in less than half a day. By canoe this journey can—and should—easily take five or six days.

Why do *I* keep coming? There is an anecdote about "madmen" in India, who were tied to trees near the water's edge. It was believed that the sound of running water could untangle the knots in their minds and help them regain sanity.

You don't even have to tie me down.

The view splits open in front of my craft, and there is no hint of the sandstone wonders waiting downstream. Purple-and-white-banded hills of volcanic ash crowd a low horizon. The chill of fall puts a silencing finger to nature's lips; no sounds but the dipping of my paddle and the murmur of the river sliding over gravel bars interfere with the evening's stillness. Russet serviceberry bushes set off the gold lace of tamarisks. Every other bend already rests in shade, and the air feels colder there. A solitary bat sidles up to the salmon-colored belly of the sky. Its curlicues seem erratic, but link dots of insect prey.

At last light I land next to Crystal Geyser, not a natural geyser, but rather the abandoned drill hole of a barren oil well several thousand feet deep. At unpredictable intervals, when enough pressure from carbon dioxide has built up, seep water erupts from the ground. As I set up camp, I strain for the spitting and rushing of this capricious fountain. But only a trickle leaks from the encrusted orifice.

During dinner, while the moon still hides bashfully behind a bluff, a pulsing—mixed with a deeper, splattering noise—suddenly augments the hissing of my stove. Water begins to leap down miniature terraces that are the result of mineral deposits from the well. The raw stench of petroleum wafts through the air. Crystal Geyser is stirring. Its shroud flutters in the pale light, rising and falling and rising again. As the pressure mounts, the release spikes upward thirty feet, reminiscent of artillery shells hitting water. The show only lasts a few minutes and never reaches Old Faithful grandeur. Still, not bad for an unnatural wonder. The column collapses one last time. I feel like clapping and cheering, but hesitate to disturb the night's limpid silence.

To my dismay, I realize over breakfast next morning that I forgot a coffee filter. Two weeks without caffeine? No way! Physical hardship is one thing, but this is suffering most unnecessary. I quickly improvise a filter from a piece of fly screen cut from my tent. I had used one of my socks on a previous trip. The result, however, was less satisfying. Especially since I had already worn that sock for a day or two.

Although they endured deprivations of the worst kind, Powell and his men never ran out of coffee, which they relished cowboy-style. River runners plying the Colorado prefer their java muddy, just like their river: "Too thick to drink, too thin to plow." "If it doesn't dissolve the spoon, it ain't coffee," is another adage you might hear around river kitchens. Abbey was also a connoisseur of the Bean. Fond of a mucho macho pose, he used to mix fresh grounds with those from the day before, chasing this sludge with a "first breakfast beer."

Which brings up the delicate matter of mood-enhancing beverages in the great outdoors. When Powell's party wrecked the *No Name* on the middle Green River, in an idyllic place they dubbed Disaster Falls, the crew managed to save a three-gallon keg of "snakebite medicine" from the wreckage. The men had smuggled it in without the Major's knowledge. Grudgingly, still bemoaning the loss of a sextant, he allowed the drenched river rats to add the warmth of whiskey to that of a driftwood fire, near which they were drying their clothes.

Abbey on the other hand loved his liquor. He made fun of Greek philosophers of the classical period, for their vapid sophistries, as for their habit of imbibing tempered wine. Beer, wine, rum, and other assorted spirits, accompanied by a stash of the obligatory after-dinner cigars, were always part of his cargo.

To be fair, the love for controlled and uncontrolled substances runs deep in the blood of most river folks. Compared to the mule-like existence of backpackers, their life is a cruise.

I once borrowed a raft for a three-week trip through Grand Canyon. Its owner proudly pointed out that "the front drop hatch will hold two dozen six-packs of beer." It did, and there was even room left for a few gallons of headache-in-a-box. Another time, when I worked for the Marlboro "Adventure" Teams (and one time was enough), a spare motor was left behind. We filled its box with slews of brews and cartons of smokes instead.

River guides with livers the texture and size of half-deflated basketballs, litter the canyon beaches. On occasion, they can be observed drinking water, "to prevent dehydration." More likely, they are washing down their morning allotment of Alka-Seltzer, or trying to dilute last night's poison that is corroding their system.

In matters of food, Abbey showed a hedonistic streak as well. He liked to eat well and plenty: scrambled eggs, bacon "buck-sliced and by the pound," green chilies, salsa, and leftover fried potatoes. And that was just breakfast. He scorned the "viscous gray slime" of oatmeal, "hardcore-hippie peanut butter, heavy as wet concrete," and other vegetarian classics on which I largely subsist, as "pussy food." An omnivore with a gargantuan appetite for all life has to offer, he would probably also have disapproved of the Major's Spartan lifestyle.

Abbey hated cows so much, it seems he wanted to exterminate the species, pound by pound, steak by steak. But he also dressed Western, rode range outside of Moab, and preferred ranching to strip-mining. He was a man of many contradictions, a man after my own taste.

Only the occasional can of peaches, fresh bighorn sheep, or beaver soup (the latter received mixed reviews) enlivened the Powell expedition's monotonous fare of beans, bannock, and bacon that quickly turned rancid. Far from potential re-supplies, Powell was less concerned with variety than with the amounts and freshness of their staples, which were frequently soaked by the river's whims:

> *July 18. The day is spent in obtaining the time and spreading our rations, which we find are badly injured. The flour has been wet and dried so many times that it is all musty and full of hard lumps. We make a sieve of mosquito netting and run our flour through it, losing more than 200 pounds by the process. Our losses, by the wrecking of the "No Name" and by various mishaps since, together with the amount thrown away today, leave us little more than two months' supplies, and to make them last thus long we must be fortunate enough to lose no more.*

And I thought I was going to market the "Bug Net Filter™" as my own invention!

I shall not discuss Abbey's sex life here—mostly for lack of juicy details. He was not so kind regarding Henry David Thoreau, who was only ever "betrothed to all of Nature," and whose Puritanism he disdained. Suffice to say, that for Ed sex was "the only realm of primordial adventure still open to most of us." And yet, behind the facade of an obsessive philanderer and bearded satyr hid a romantic, for whom commitment was as foreign as the rocks of the moon. He just could not settle down. Until he met his last wife, Clarke, and began the messy business of dying.

As far as we know, the Major stayed faithful to his wife (who was also his cousin) Emma Dean, even naming his lead boat after her. She was probably much calmed during his prolonged absences by the knowledge that no nubile female was within hundreds of miles of her husband, and that he had his nose too close to the rocks to even notice much of anything else.

When I push off in the morning, the geyser again raises and dips its flag in a salute. In passing, I get a good look at its calcifications. A rust-red tongue of micro-ledges laps at the river, reminding me of congealed gravy.

The air is ripe with the scent of decaying leaves and mud. Once in a while, the harsh calls of geese, or the slapping of a beaver's tail breaks the river's quiet demeanor. With snappy J-strokes I warm up and propel the twelve-foot plastic craft into the main current. I give the load a quick once-over, to make sure the rubberized river bags are in place and secure.

Since he was a practical man, Powell would perhaps have admired this modern gear. The heavy oak boats of the expedition were built to his specifications, since no predecessor existed for this kind of craft or endeavor. They had waterproof storage compartments fore and aft, as well as a center deck. The oarsmen were awkwardly facing upstream and had to be directed by a second crew member, who operated a sweep oar fixed to the stern for steering. Although they lined or portaged most of the serious rapids, the boats were frequently swamped and damaged. They required frequent caulking, or even the replacement of entire planks and oars.

But hardship was the Major's métier, and he would have drawn the line at portable toilets. By now, many commercial outfitters have replaced the infamous "groover," an army-issue rocket-launcher box stenciled *Caution—Explosives*. These days, boats carry a stainless steel "thunder jug" that comes with a cushy seat.

Abbey too, was much less discerning in his choice of equipment than many a modern gear fetishist. He launched anything with paddles or oars, as long as it was big enough to drag a mesh bag to chill beer in. Ed's rides included "garbage scows," inflatable sportyaks, and old army assault rafts: sausage-skinned, rubber "baloney boats." Once, at a drugstore en route to Glen Canyon, he bought a bathtub-sized vinyl dinghy, a craft that needed continuous pumping. On the same occasion, he used a gas-station roadmap to guide him and a friend on a float trip of almost two weeks' duration. If Powell embodied the heroic type lionized by a Victorian populace, Abbey played trickster and visionary to a jaded postmodern audience. But he could also rough it with the best.

My ideal has always been to wield the pen as well as the paddle. This is why the man whose book I carry became a role model. My battered copy wears the "Local Author" sticker of the Moab public library, proof that oddballs, seasonal migrants, and eastern transplants *can* do well for themselves.

He has been compared to "Coyote in the Maze of Words," and Abbey did indeed have a nose for stories, a keen ear for dialogue, and a wicked sense of humor. Scratching his shaggy beard, he kept digging for lyrical morsels and metaphor. He pissed all over authority. Accusations of being "sexist" or "racist" stung his hide even less than parasites trying to feed off his fame. Unfettered by the chains of other literary top dogs, he joined the chorus of souls wild and free; he laughed in the faces of bureaucrats, nipped at the heels of critics and hypocrites. He was out to overturn the garbage cans of civilization. Some have called his sense of humor "low." I consider it earthy. Unpretentious. How could anyone love playing with language and not appreciate a pun? I know that Ed would have greeted places like Junes Bottom or Mollie's Nipple or the Bishop's Prick with thigh-slapping mirth.

I burn with questions for this audacious trickster. How did you dare jump from Jim Bridger to Nietzsche in two sentences and pull it off? How could you fuse redneck speech with lyricisms and move me to tears? (Well, almost.) In your writing you berated the "self-conscious cult of meditation, retreat and renewal" as a sign of lives lived in quiet desperation. But *what else* were you seeking on this autumnal stretch of river?

He only smiles that coyote smile, licking his chops.

It was the fact that the writer and man were nevertheless two halves of the same mold that impressed me the most. Abbey's actions were as unbridled and direct as his words. Rants against the military-industrial complex and nation-state meshed seamlessly with the felling of billboards and the pulling of survey stakes, while wearing a government uniform. His stoic acceptance of death and a renegade funeral in the desert spoke volumes.

I only fell in love with the redrock desert the year friends laid him to rest in his ratty sleeping bag, amidst ocotillo and rattlesnakes, the wailing of bagpipes, sounds of clinking bottles, crying, and lovemaking. *Desert Solitaire* primed my desire to become ashes rather than dust. I ditched a "career" and became a transient guide, a student of chipmunks, a sagebrush scholar instead. I was a curmudgeon already, but I picked up pen and paper.

Things have not been the same since.

According to Abbey's assessment that "all the greatest writers challenge us to change our lives," Powell was not a great writer. That was never his goal. Political ambition, self-promotion, and the broadcasting of his discoveries fueled his report. The Major *did* have a lyrical vein. But his homemade education as the son of a Methodist minister, and his work as a teacher and principal at a public school in Illinois, marked him for government work rather than literary or scientific greatness.

Twenty miles from town, the debris of our civilization still disgraces the riverbanks. Dilapidated cabins lean at drunken angles. Hollows gape where windows and doors used to be. Sagging barbed-wire fences fail to contain the wind. Water pumps, old mining equipment, and an abandoned car gather rust, slowly reverting to earth.

At port side, Dellenbaugh Butte sails placidly by—a gigantic layered-chocolate cake. With the unconcerned straightforwardness of most explorers that grows from arrogance or ignorance, Powell put place-names along this river as if he had created it: Labyrinth, Stillwater, Bowknot Bend, Tower Park, Fort Bottom, Trin Alcove. Occasionally, he lapsed into poetry, at Cleopatra's Chair, or passing through the Gates of Lodore. Posthumously, the Major lent his good name to the atrocity of "Lake" Powell, more correctly—if less widely—known as Glen Canyon Reservoir.

Although Abbey believed names to be useful mnemonic devices, he doubted their ability to capture the essence of things: "Is there any reason out here, for any name?" he asked. "These huge walls and giant towers and vast mazy avenues of stone resist attempts at verbal reduction." Sure. But *all* nature writing is verbal reduction. Names can enrich a place by adding new layers of meaning, as long as the pointing finger is not mistaken for the moon.

Abbey did not leave any names on the land, and has never been officially honored with a feature named after him. When will we finally begin to immortalize *writers* instead of explorers, two-bit politicians, and cowpokes in our western landscapes? And when will we start calling a lake a lake and a reservoir a reservoir?

With the same right as Powell, who re-christened the hump that was locally known as Anvil Butte after one of his crew, and disregarding Abbey's concerns, I bestow Ed's name upon the brown outcrop.

The Major's dusty prose style was most likely shaped by his training as a naturalist, and more specifically, a geologist. (For a rare example of flashy geological description, I recommend Clarence Dutton's *Tertiary History of the Grand Canyon District: The Panorama from Point Sublime*.) I don't think there is a single wisecrack, pun, or even bon mot to be found in all of Powell's tomes. He was a collector of facts and later became a collector and cataloguer of Native American artifacts as head of the newly founded Bureau of American Ethnology. A hardheaded empiricist to the bone, he was constantly fiddling with sextant, barometer, or theodolite, fixing the expedition's position, determining the river gradient, or recording the weather. On rare occasions, he could wax poetic about the natural beauty through which they glided:

> *Away to the west are lines of cliffs and ledges of rock—*
> *not such ledges as the reader may have seen where the*
> *quarryman splits his blocks, but ledges from which the*

*gods might quarry mountains that, rolled out on the plain below, would stand a lofty range.*

Much to the chagrin of his rustic crew, he recited sonnets and read from romantic novels, presiding over them in an armchair bolted to the center deck of the *Emma Dean*, while the boats were lashed together on stretches of flat water. Thus, though extremely scary, the rapids brought temporary relief to his men.

Abbey, on the other hand, was trained in the liberal arts, and had written a thesis on the philosophy of anarchism. Although he rejected the label "nature writer," selling himself and his work short as "environmental journalism," his writing sparkles with poignant observations and descriptions of the natural world.

Where the two *really* parted ways was in the meaning of meaning.

Powell firmly believed that geological theory could explain what loomed before his eyes, without any residue. Abbey was forever haunted by "the disturbing, heart-opening quality" of the land. "To grasp the 'meaning' of it all" he expostulated, "we require a science with room for more than data and information, a science that includes sympathy for the object under study, and more than sympathy, love." Tender words for a beer-swilling anarchist! He even went so far as to ascribe rights to rocks and non-human beings, anticipating tenets of ecosystem justice. To truly understand the "suchness of things," Ed recommended "intuitive, qualitative, not merely quantitative understanding," based upon "prolonged contact and interaction." This is unusually subdued prose for Ed, and roughly translates as follows: get out of your damn cars. Get bloodied, blistered, tired, and beaten up. Let the desert fry your brains; let alkaline water flush the rot of civilization from your guts. Prostrate yourselves like true believers.

And as your brow touches the ground, you just might get a whiff of the Great Mystery.

By noon, a cloud blanket has palled the sky. Drizzle dimples the water. The pinkish cast of greasewood-stippled dunes announces the Entrada Sandstone, whose cubist faces are streaked black. Light sheets the world in thick, substantial layers, lending the cliffs an underwater quality. A stiff upstream breeze crimps the broad back of the current; it tussles with cottonwoods, robs them of their autumnal glory and me of my strength.

As I draw deeper into geological time, the half-domes, striped tapestries, and blind arches of the Navajo formation eventually mark the transition to Labyrinth Canyon.

Infinitudes of paddle strokes later, the welcome harbor of Trin Alcove cleaves the rocky embankments. While I unload the canoe, I decide to lay over, to give my knotted tendons, shoulders, and back a chance to hang out and relax with a tired mind. The day's impressions roll around in my head like pebbles in a flood that subsides only reluctantly.

Night strikes swiftly at this time of year. After dinner, trying to stretch the day, I withdraw to the coziness of my down bag with headlamp, nightcap, and my readings. I contemplate, which of the two men, whose dreams I have been tracking down this river as part of my own, would have made the better travel companion.

Tension was slowly mounting to a breaking point, as Powell's party proceeded through Grand Canyon. It has been carefully edited from the Major's report, but is more than just hinted at in the diaries of various crew members. One of his men lost a treasured watch on loan from Powell and did not hear the end of it. In the lower part of the gorge, the final rift occurred. At a place afterward known as Separation Canyon, three members of the expedition opted to hike out. They were tired of bad food, tired of cold and wet clothes, tired of the Major's dark temper. They were also intimidated by more daunting rapids churning ahead. After ascending to the Kaibab Plateau, this party was ambushed and killed by Shivits Paiute near the North Rim. The rest of the expedition floated to safety and a glorious homecoming.

Studying a photo of Powell, one gets the impression that he would eat nails for breakfast or could shave the whiskers off you with his gaze. The blocky forehead, bushy eyebrows, and scowling stare reveal a driven and strong-willed personality. The statuesque beard framing this face is shot through with silver and would hide any smile that happened to stumble upon the stern countenance.

A portrait of the late Edward Abbey shows a man with similar facial hair, and the bulbous nose he ascribed to the transcendentalists. But whereas Powell's wrinkled brow intimidates, Abbey's finely lined face speaks of compassion (if not for everybody) and a good dose of weariness. At the same time, crow's feet and a glint in the eyes betray a capacity for mischief.

Although Ed Abbey had his occasional tiff with friends—who called him "Abbey," "Cactus Ed," "Frijol Viejo," or worse—he was just as quick to make up again. Even under the leveling influence of the frontier, Powell always remained "the Major" to his men, carefully maintaining class barriers erected by the Victorian mentality and an institutional background.

Before my thoughts turn sluggish and my eyelids start drooping, I reach a conclusion: I would have rather gone boating with bristly, brilliant, moody, polemic, boisterous, troubled Ed—if for no other reasons than that he was the better paddler and would have brought beer.

I rise early next morning, for an exploration up Three Canyon, heeding Ed's exhortation that "ten hours is too long to spend curled in a sleeping bag." My coffee tastes strange. When I check my supplies, I find that the crystal-clear water with which I filled my water bags yesterday is alkaline and really undrinkable. Thank god I did not cut my nightcap with that.

Upon my return, I am shocked to find that the Waltons have moved in next-door, dogs, kids, and all. Shouts and thumping from a boom box pour from the alcove, and canyon walls throw back the noise. Perhaps you were right, Ed. The canyons and rivers *have* become cluttered with the junk, voices, and smells of too many people. But the desire to be heard in these titanic gorges, to assure ourselves that we have substance against this vacuum of mute indifference, weighs heavily on all of us. "Now and then we whistle or shout, or discharge a pistol, to listen to the reverberations among the cliffs," reads an entry from Powell's journal dated July 15, 1869.

Since I cannot sit still for long, and the day is still young, I scale the rim for a raven's-eye view of Trin Alcove. Without warning, it springs open in the gray, denuded plateau, like a busted bank vault, or Aladdin's cave. Old gold and emeralds of cottonwood and willow leaves sparkle from the depths. Their glimmer is overlaid with the copper tone of turning oaks. Rubies of gilia and amethyst asters spill across the canyon bottom, though too distant to be spotted from my roost. Other gems lie concealed in the shade of walls decked in pink and blue-black ribbons. A luxurious carpet of mossy green absorbs every sound. Above all billow draperies of silver-lined clouds.

Back at the sandbar, I still feel exhilarated and grateful for yet another jewel of a day stolen from death.

The second night in this place, a storm shoulders its way through the canyon. Thunder ricochets from the walls, like boulders bouncing in a bowling alley of giants. Rain whips the ground into foam and threshes my home-away-from-home. Separated from the violence only by a flimsy layer of nylon, I feel thin-skinned and small. Was it something I wrote, Ed? Or are you just having a good time, trundling rocks off the rim, like you did on the San Juan?

The new day looks innocent enough, as I pack up my sodden tent. My paddle blade cuts into yet another calm morning, sending miniature whirlpools upstream. The canoe's bow breaks mirror images of cliffs, clouds, and sky, leaving shards reflecting eternity in my wake. Back-lit by the low sun, herds of bubbles migrate downstream. They always follow the deepest channel. Labyrinth Canyon owes its name to the complacent nature of rivers with low gradients and velocity. As the stream procrastinates, it lays down its trademark meanders. Initially suspended, sediment drops out, creating sandbars and shallows where the current slows to a crawl at the inside of a bend.

Deciphering the calligraphy of river channels is essential, especially in a low water year such as this one. On any calm day, watch out for ripples, or the change in reflections that betray the presence of shallows. Listen for the final warning of your paddle scraping the bottom. Then, step into the toe-numbing river, look foolish, and drag your boat off the gravel. I have hiked many a mile of the Colorado, just another white man coming down the river with a plastic boat in tow. As the old river guide joke says: "We scrape to make a living."

Of all the canyons crosshatching the Colorado Plateau, Labyrinth and Stillwater probably most closely resemble the grandeur of Glen Canyon before the cursed dam cut off its lifeblood. A subdued roiling courses through horseshoe curves. Bottomlands beckon with cottonwood shade. Side canyons and amphitheaters unfold like hidden blossoms, while sandstone escarpments tower, in shapes even Antoni Gaudí could not have envisioned.

And yet, no Music Temple, no Sentinel Rock, no Cathedral in the Desert, Dungeon Canyon, or Hidden Passage remains, to snare us with the magic of its name.

The River Post Office at Bowknot Bend provides the backdrop for my next place of impermanent residence. Only a gooseneck of land prevents the river from falling back on itself. While the turbid flood wheels about for three hundred fifty degrees, it travels nearly five miles to gain less than one-quarter. An even longer loop follows immediately, almost completing a figure eight. As the vulture flies is not as the river runner runs, in this squirming country.

Atop the skinny peninsula sits a register where boaters can leave their names, together with messages for following parties. The campsites perch on a bench above the meander, nearly perfect, offering expansive views and soil firm enough to stay put in a storm. Even the yellow fur of the tamarisk pest, which lines most of the sweeping bench lands of this section, is missing.

Tonight I am spared the hit-and-run of a thunderstorm. A single cumulus cloud lurks on the edge of a star-dusted sky, barely peeping over the canyon rim. Once in a while it flickers from within, maintaining an eerie silence; the heat lightning outlines every contour and curve, as if in a snapshot. Since the air chills quickly, I decide to make my own insignificant contribution to the great pulsing in the sky. Flames catch in an instant. They greedily devour the brittle driftwood sticks, which I feed them.

I let the journey up to this point drift by my mind's eye. One by one, days have disappeared down the river, like so much flotsam. The put-in at Green River already seems lifetimes away. A simple existence, with no other urge than to keep rolling, is the river's great gift. It is hard to imagine that I ever lived for different rewards, that such a life is even possible.

❖❖❖

Above a rock ledge at the mouth of Hellroaring Canyon, a fellow traveler felt compelled to inform the world of his passing. The inscription, scratched into sandstone varnish, has been badly vandalized. It reads "D. Julien," above "1836" and "3 Mai." It is flanked by the outline of a canoe-style craft with a single mast and an enigmatic winged eye or sun.

Denis Julien was a trapper from St. Louis, who left several inscriptions in this area. One of them, in lower Cataract Canyon, now lies buried underneath the stagnation that is Glen Canyon Reservoir. Its location in a place that formerly could only have been reached at high water levels and by boat, has led river historians to the conclusion that Julien possibly preceded Powell in his descent of that boiling cauldron of whitewater.

Mysteriously, some of the lower inscriptions predate those found upstream, and it almost appears that Julien traveled against the current. On flat water, this would have been possible with strong upstream winds and a sail-assisted boat like the one depicted here.

The canoe has become the emblem of a fur trade long dominated by French-Canadian voyageurs. In bark canoes inspired by Algonquin Indian designs, they followed the arteries of dry western reaches in search of the brown gold. During the heyday of the skin business, between the 1820s and 1830s, about one hundred thousand beaver pelts per year were converted into elegant top hats. This industry quickly pushed North America's largest rodent to the brink of extinction.

At the same time, the fur boom contributed to the opening and commercialization of territories, which were still largely controlled by Spain and Mexico. William Wolfskill explored the San Juan River, northwestern New Mexico, and southern Colorado in 1822. Jedediah Smith hunted and trapped near

Zion in 1826. These two men were the first Anglo-Americans in southern Utah. In 1824, the Pattie brothers, Sylvester and Ohio, gazed into the mind-bending abyss of Grand Canyon; they followed the Little Colorado and Wind River all the way to Santa Fe, endpoint of the Old Spanish Trail, and to Taos, center of the southwestern fur trade.

*Castor canadensis* was just barely spared the fate of ivory-billed woodpecker and passenger pigeon. Luckily, around 1850 the European craze for men's hats made from rich, sleek fur unaccountably shifted to headgear fashioned from imported Chinese silk.

The wholesale loss of beavers altered the nature of desert rivers and creeks. Without their wickerwork dams, wetlands and marshes shrank or disappeared from the upper reaches, reducing habitat for other species. Long-trapped sediment washed downstream. Water temperatures increased. Feeder streams became more volatile in the absence of natural reservoirs. They turned from year-round water sources into fickle runs cutting arroyos and gullies, or into mere trickles, depending on the whims of flood and drought cycles.

Abbey had a soft spot for mountain men and what he saw as their unfettered, down-to-earth lives. Joining Native American bison hunters and Jeffersonian yeoman farmers, they became the antithesis of a debasing, government-controlled urban-industrial civilization and its economic dealings. This however, is a literary conceit that goes at least as far back as the Enlightenment.

Reality was slightly less romantic. The rugged individualists, who were frequently "married" to native women and roamed from the Mississippi to the mouth of the Colorado, from the frozen subarctic to the Gila River, acted only as pathfinders and ambassadors of a homogenizing, profit-hungry society. Knowingly or unknowingly, they introduced their hosts to firearms and bad booze, to venereal and epidemic diseases. They acted as ambassadors for the glittering misery of the free-market economy. A connection seems to exist between the buckskin-clad dropouts of yore and a current of contemporary seekers: the craving for more and more remote places, which are quickly tainted by our desires.

Below Mineral Bottom, cottonwoods crowd the bottomlands, shading splendid campsites. But impenetrable thickets of tamarisk wall them off as efficiently as barbed-wire fences.

On his journey down the Colorado and Green, Powell did not have to deal with this bane of southwestern gallery forests. The fast-growing salt cedar was introduced only shortly before the turn of the century, in various species from the eastern Mediterranean, North Africa, and China. As an ornamental, it also provided shade and helped to control riverbank erosion. Except for the endangered southwest willow flycatcher, this tree provides only limited wildlife habitat. It is tolerant of, and even increases, the salt content of soils already infamous for their salinity. It thus crowds out plants that are native to riparian corridors, like willows and cottonwoods. A water guzzler to boot, the feathery-leaved growth can absorb its own weight of water per day, drastically lowering stream and spring levels. In some cases, it manages to suck water sources entirely dry.

When I finally locate a gap in the green defense belt, a vicious mudflat bars the way. I unlace my boots and, barefoot, knee-deep in cold muck, haul my boat to the steep bank. Unloading, I slip and am half-swallowed by a lip-smacking mess. It takes some serious bushwhacking to find a place where I can wash myself without stepping or sliding into the slop again.

I hike up a side canyon, in search of water fit to drink. Not far up the drainage, a hunter with bow and arrow has been pecked into a boulder, next to images of bighorn sheep. Depictions of bow hunting are rather uncommon in the prehistoric rock art of this area, but petroglyphs decorating walls near the mouths of tributaries are not. Like billboards along the sides of a highway, they are hard to miss. I wonder if they could have had a similar function. "Hey—excellent sheep hunting. Only three miles up this exit!" Or did they advertise clan territories, as is often presumed? "One more step and you will end up with sharp objects in your skin!" The images do not tell us. Whereas many aspects of the material culture of the Fremont have been reconstructed from archaeological finds, their beliefs and social practices shall remain intriguing—perhaps forever, and fortunately so.

Rain pummels the canyon all night. At some point, shivering and soaked, I find myself digging a flood trench around the tent with a butter knife.

The new day breaks over a river shrouded in golden mist. After launching, I glide by a beaver on shore, which is too busy to notice me. In the deep quiet to which I have become accustomed by now, I hear it gnaw on a willow branch. Slick fur glistens darkly in the sun, insulating a body that has been streamlined over millennia by the current itself. A great blue heron takes flight. Wings bat air in slow motion, like a tablecloth that is shaken out. In the takeoff, the outer primary feathers of the reptilian bird sough and almost touch the wing tips of its mirrored twin.

I stop at Anderson Bottom, to scout for another panel of rock inscriptions. The stream has abandoned one of its meanders here, creating a shortcut. The wide loop of this rincón with its fertile alluvial soil provided a perfect place to live and forage in. Shaded by an overhang, amid snakes and human outlines of an earlier provenance, a Fremont warrior brandishes a large decorated shield. Only his stylized head and legs show above and below the curved rim, unprotected.

Between bows, arrows, and shields and MX intercontinental missiles, not much seems to have changed. We know from archaeological discoveries that contemporaries of Fremont hunters known as "Enemy Ancestors" or Anasazi, committed atrocities worthy of a Stalin, Hitler, or Pol Pot. How does this resonate with the idyll of an unspoiled people hunting, weaving baskets, feasting, fasting for visions, incising murals, and living in harmony with their surroundings, which Abbey also liked to conjure in his writings? I guess there was room for decency, creativity, and cooperation in the "New World"—just as there was a Schweitzer, Einstein, or Bach in the old.

Near Anderson Bottom, the fine-grained White Rim Sandstone rises to frame the entrance to Stillwater Canyon. On top of a crumbling bluff, I lose myself in a dizzying view. Sculpted buttes of the Wingate formation with fanciful names like Candlestick Tower or Buttes of the Cross have been split from the massive block of land delineated by the converging arms of the Green and Colorado Rivers. The vertical fluting of these sandstone monuments rests on rainbow shoulders of Chinle, at whose feet tawny hills of Moenkopi unroll. A few stories below, the dull lead of the river shows, entrenched in the White Rim like a heat coil in butter. Shadows cast by a flighty sky play over a landscape dominated by horizons. Veils of distant rain blue parts of the vista, while searchlights of angels slant through the roving clouds, adding depth and mood to this corroded world.

Farther downstream, the Maze entices with all its stern beauty. Smooth sandstone at the river's level has by now given way to the rough-and-tumble of older limestone formations. A fire that could have been started by a careless camper ravaged the mouth of a side drainage yawning into the main corridor. Scrofulous lumps disfigure charred cottonwood skeletons, and the burned flat bristles with tumbleweed and desolation.

I know that the upper part of this canyon, hidden above a huge dryfall, remains picturesque and pristine. It is supposedly the only canyon within this national park that has never been grazed by cattle. After the author of a hiking guide lauded it as the gem of the Canyonlands, it became popular overnight. Like so many cows, backpackers quickly trampled the secluded oasis. The National Park Service had to close it, to preserve a microenvironment that could yield useful information about pre-ranching conditions. True to the spirit of the Wilderness Act, this hideaway now exists "untrammeled by man" or woman. Its hidden presence raises an uncomfortable question. Do we love our wild places enough to leave some alone?

Sometime past noon, the brooding sky bursts, unleashing a gully washer. Water spouts from every cleft in the rimrock, shoots out in graceful arcs, before plummeting and vaporizing upon impact twelve hundred feet below. Cascades bound from ledge to ledge and stripe the faces of cliffs. On the talus slopes, boulders gleam like Japanese lacquer boxes, vegetation takes on an almost tropical tint. Long after the rain stops, the gorge is still ringing with the eloquence of water rushing off washboard plateaus.

Tonight is Halloween. To dry my damp clothes and keep the ghosts of the departed at bay, I gather kindling and start a small fire. Entranced by the gyrations of flames, I barely notice the bearded figure just inside the cocoon of light. He wears a gray felt hat. Leather vest. Scuffed boots. I recognize him immediately.

"What the...? You scared me." No reply, but an impish grin plays on his face. Perhaps it is only a trick of the flickering light.

"Is the Major here, too? Where is he?"

"I dunno, off somewhere, mapping and measuring this hell-hole of a place." The voice is as smooth as river gravel, with a tinge of East Coast.

"Where are you?"

"Here."

"No, I mean—"

"I'm not at liberty to tell. But I sure miss John Barleycorn, a good see-gar and my river, *muy colorado.*"

"Here, have one on me." I hold my mug of gullet warmer out to him. He reaches for it, and his hand passes through.

"Damn!"

"What about—"

"Sorry, kid, gotta go."

"Wait Ed, wait!" But the specter slowly dissolves.

Goosebumps run up and down my spine like cold fingers. When Abbey proclaimed that any writer worth his salt should raise hackles until long after his death, he probably did not mean it like this.

In a theatrical gesture, I pour a good swig of whiskey into the flames, which turn blue and hiss and spit at me. From deep within my sleeping bag, I listen for voices. Only the jabbering of insomniac geese by the river punctures the night.

By the time I approach the Y-junction where two rivers kiss, water from a hole in the keel sloshes around my feet. This is the result of scraping through one shallow channel too many. I cannot suppress a chuckle, however, recalling Abbey's first boating adventure. In the preface to the volume I carry, he recounts stealing a wooden cement mixing trough and sinking it, with himself and his brother as crew, in the frigid waters of Crooked Crick, west Pennsylvania.

The Confluence is a place of great serenity. Over the years, I have dredged a hoard of memories from the two streams that merge in the shadow of Junction Butte. Like the contrasting tones of these currents, they momentarily run side by side with the hopes, dreams, worries, follies, infatuations, and deceptions of all those who ever hunted, explored, grew up and grew old, made love, died, worked, and played within sight of these waters. For an instant, the voices remain distinct. They boil to the surface, sink, swirl, and eddy, to finally blend into one eminent sibilance.

The Confluence is beginnings and endings. Only a brief pause, and the mad dash toward the sea, toward oblivion, resumes. Excitement and the worlds of Cataract and Grand Canyon still wait below.

This middle-aged river throws itself with renewed vigor into whirlpools and ledges, against house rocks and steep banks, battling confinement. Its convulsions splinter driftwood and oars as carelessly as the egos of confident boaters. In the long run, even the dams that block its way cannot resist. Only ruins of broken steel and concrete will cling to the river's flanks, fallen monuments of yet another imperial dream.

Powell continued from here, unable to ignore the siren song of adventure. "We have an unknown distance yet to run, an unknown river to explore," reads his terse journal entry. Abbey returned to Moab by powerboat—quite out of style—"back to what they call Reality." Perhaps pressed for time, he saved the thrills of Cataract Canyon for a different trip. I too, have to leave its opportunities for some other time. I stash my boat in a willow thicket nearby, where it can be retrieved next spring.

The two men, whose words and deeds offered succor and guidance, have long preceded me on the ultimate journey. I fervently wish for their respective brands of courage. I hope when my time comes to embark, I will be able to let go, to entrust myself to the current. I may not be saved, but shall be safe on its wide shoulders. Knowing it will carry me. Knowing it will deliver me—back to the source.

Before I load up and face the back-numbing trail ahead, I pull the tab off my last can of Tecate and toast the Major, Ed, and the River.

# 9

# THE UNSPEAKABLE BEAST

*"I am like a bear.*
*I hold up my hands*
*Waiting for the sun to rise."*

—*from a Ute song*

I ARRIVE ON TOP OF THE BEARS EARS AS THE LIGHT DIES, JUST in time to watch the copper orb of the sun roll into the sky's well. It quickly sinks into purple depths. The buttes are awash with the color of blood, shed when time itself was still young. I watch as blue shadows reach for the base of this desert outcrop. From up here, it is possible to make out the stencil-cut silhouettes of landmarks in three adjacent states. The transparency of this evening allows a glimpse into the soul of creation itself.

Before I spread out my sleeping bag for ascetic bedding, I recite the familiar names and receive the surrounding tableau like a blessing. Peaks of the La Sal and Abajo ranges border the view far to the north. Sleeping Ute Mountain reclines above Colorado, edged by mares' tails that brush the eastern horizon. My eyes flit over the undulations of Comb Ridge bisecting the southeastern quadrant, then snag on the San Juan Mountains' blunted saw. Due south, Navajo Mountain protects the heart of a reservation in Arizona, and the life ways of a people molded from brick-red soils. And toward sunset, the Henries lend a splendid backdrop to the clog-shaped feature at the head of Woodenshoe Canyon, my destination.

Next morning I roll up camp early, after a quick, cold breakfast of oats mixed with water and powdered milk. A washed-out sun, hung over from staying up late, hides behind haze from a fire that is turning the pine-stippled plateaus of Mesa Verde into ashes. Light teases the ground with nimble fingers. A few hours from now it will strike with iron gauntlets. The West is going up in smoke again this summer, and for weeks, the mercury has quivered near the 105-degree mark, with rain scarce and scattered. Last winter's snow blanket—long since unraveled by the solar embrace—had been a letdown. It left the earth parched and lean, the brush crackling like old snakeskins. Animals, plants, people, the very core of the land, now yearn for the madness of rushing water.

To escape the spiraling heat, I trudge across Elk Ridge, plunge into pools of Douglas firs, ponderosa pines, Gambel oaks, and quaking aspens. Before the path is swallowed by the gradually deepening draw, I turn for a last glance at the Bears Ears. Notched and rusty like an old gun sight, the Wingate-capped pair of clipped buttes straddles the ridge as part of the Monument Upwarp. It is possibly the most intriguing landform carved from Dark Canyon Plateau.

During the traumatic 1860s, with Colonel Kit Carson and his Ute mercenaries hard on his heels, Kaa'yeełii, a brother of Diné leader Manuelito, found a hideout not too far from here. Five or six hogans hugged a stony dell, at a place called Naahootso: Place-Across-the-River-to-Escape-from-the-Enemy. The twin buttes guard an imaginary line that runs from Comb Ridge to

Moonwater, separating Ute tribal territory east of it from Dinétah, the "Land of the Diné." The story of Changing Bear Maiden is forever linked to this place, in what author Terry Tempest Williams has called "a sacred visualization, a way of echoing experience."

According to this myth, a young Diné woman turned evil and devious by marrying Old Man Coyote, the classical trickster and lecher of southwestern folklore. Shape-shifting into a bear, she turned against and killed her brothers, except one. He eventually managed to track down, kill, and dismember her. (If your skin crawls at this, remember some of the Grimm brothers' grisly tales.) The scattered body parts and organs turned into scores of animals and plants, many of them edible and useful to the Diné. The highly nutritious nuts of the pinyon pine, for instance, are an embodiment of Changing Bear Maiden's nipples; the severed head, tossed away by the brother, morphed into the Bears Ears. Nearby Comb Wash is a furrow he dug with his knife to prevent her poisonous blood from reaching him.

Medicinal plants used to cure witchcraft are gathered near the site to this day. It is also visited to treat women's depression in the Mountainway ceremony. The bear in turn, is now considered a powerful medicine animal and healer, a role supported by the belief that a wounded one can find roots and herbs to heal itself. Health and harmony, physical as well as mental, are thus rooted in land that has been fertilized with the humus of oral history.

Like the song lines of Australian Aborigines explored by Bruce Chatwin, mythical ancestors left traces and legacies on this broken earth. Stories set in stone keep the past and its lessons alive. With every retelling, bonds between people and places and their non-human residents are strengthened, codes of moral conduct reinforced. Examples of anthropomorphic attitudes toward landscapes even survive in the Judeo-Christian tradition: we still speak of the head or mouth of a canyon, of the face of a cliff, the arm of a river, or a mountain's shoulder and flank. But these are only metaphors, not myths we center our lives by.

From the Arctic Circle to the desert Southwest, Native people have bowed to the spiritual and physical prowess of bears, acknowledging that the fates of both "races" are closely entwined. Pueblo Indians who belong to the bear clan trace their descent directly from this animal. In exchange for songs, incantations, and prayers that rise from sun-blasted plazas or the secrecy of kivas, these humans enjoy special protection by their totemic ancestor.

I have repeatedly listened to tales about intermarriage, about people who were raised by bears and inherited their medicine powers. Like the womb, or death, the bear den has often symbolized transformation. Tied closely to the ability of some people to assume animal shape, it reminds us that the boundaries between different states of existence are permeable.

In an era of newspapers and television, scandals and election campaigns, nobody really believes that "sticks and stones may break your bones, but words will never hurt you." Akin to shamans, writers understand only too well, how the primal worldview accepts the ominous powers of language without question. Words can conjure objects with all their associated qualities and repercussions; the knowledge of true identities empowers. At the same time, it may wake a destructive potential that slumbers in the name-bearer. (That is why Rumpelstiltskin threw such a fit when he was found out.) Casting a spell and spelling a name are merely two facets of a single reality, glittering precariously.

It is this existential dread, rather than just respect for the animal's physical strength, that is acknowledged in a Navajo song:

> *"There is danger when I move my feet.*
> *I am a gray bear.*

*When I walk, where I step, lightning*
*flies from me.*
*Where I walk, one to be feared I am...*
*There is danger where I walk."*

The Paiute strive not to offend the bear's spirit and to avoid possible paybacks of disease or bad luck. They use a circumlocution, "maternal grandmother," rather than its true name, when speaking to or about the animal. With this move, a force that cannot be controlled otherwise finds its paws shackled by kinship. One does not shed blood that is shared, unless in self-preservation, or corrupted by a trickster.

Similarly, the Diné employed the honorific *shash*, and addressed the Fine Young Chief Roaming the Woods cautiously, when they had to hunt him in times of need. Their approach was always marked by utmost respect and humility; and they disposed of the animal's remains ceremoniously.

Not even English or the other Germanic languages have a word for the genus *Ursus* that is straightforward. "Bear" and "bruin" are nothing but allusions, carefully hinting at "the brown one"; the name Arthur can be traced back to the furry, hibernating clan via the Celtic *artos*; and Beowulf, the legendary Anglo-Saxon warrior-hero, is nothing but a guise of the "Beewolf," yet another attempt to beat around the bush in which the raider of hives might be lurking. The Indo-European root word (*rks*) for the Great Bear was flat-out rejected, but entered English through the backdoor of Greek. Concealed in the term "arctic," it signifies the land sleeping under the constellation of Ursa Major. Present-day Euro-Americans do not seem completely immune either, against the numinous power of the forest stalker. A fellow nature writer titled her chapter on southwestern grizzlies, "The Disappeared Ones."

In a variety of beliefs and practices, tribal people express an ambivalence of admiration and fear. For some obscure reason, ursine gourmands not only feed on, but also love to roll in the small fields where the Diné grow corn. Once an animal has stomped through a cornfield, people believe he has claimed it and no longer harvest it for their own use. Likewise, a traditional Navajo will not collect pinyon pine nuts where a bear has been gathering them. Neither will he fashion a cradleboard from the wood of a tree against which it has rubbed its itching skin.

These sentiments persist in contemporary Navajo society. At the request of the progressive faction of the tribe, the Navajo opened a sport-hunting season for black bear in the 1960s. Shortly after traditional elders vehemently protested the decision, it was closed for good.

Final evidence for the magic of bears comes in the form of prehistoric rock art panels across the Colorado Plateau. Hardly any contain depictions of the complete animal. But stylized prints of bear paws were occasionally chiseled into varnished rock skin, often with enough detail to distinguish claws, as well as front from hind feet. It almost seems as if parts have to stand for the whole of an animal considered unthinkable in its entirety.

At the bottom of Woodenshoe Canyon, crested Steller's jays scold from the canopy, sounding like rusty door hinges. The birds dip from tree to tree, slate-gray in the shade, steel blue in the sun. On its way to the Colorado, wind hurries through treetops. Gigantic pines sway in the current with grace, waltzing to inaudible tunes. The clean scent of baking earth and pine needles tickles my nostrils, birdsong my ears. Where the trees part, views of buff, bulging Cedar Mesa Sandstone come as revelations. Rock flexes its muscle into amphitheaters over a thousand feet high.

The fresh mud glaze in the streambed holds palm-sized tracks of a mountain lion, not older than a day or two. Close by, prints of a black bear grab my attention. Indented ovals of five leathery toes curve around the lobed depressions left by its foot-pads. (Grizzly toe prints are typically arranged on a straighter line. Also, the indentations from the tips of their claws are farther from the toes, indicating longer claw size.) This time, the claws have not left any marks on the ground. Perhaps the mud had nearly dried when the animal passed through. Black piles of scat of varying freshness, spiked with undigested berries, further betray the presence of the omnivorous wayfarer. Earlier, I had noticed dark scars in the white skin of aspens, where bears had climbed trunks or simply mauled them from sheer exuberance. But I did not pay much attention. Now, my senses are on red alert, scanning the vicinity with radar-like intensity. Every boulder suddenly turns into a bear, and when I flush a flock of wild turkeys from the brush, my heart skips.

This summer, black bears have ventured into the canyons and skimmed the fringes of towns. While I was loading rafts in Desolation Canyon a few weeks ago, a burly male had sauntered down the beach to within a hundred yards. He was flipping over rocks, nonchalant in his search for crayfish or other treats. And only last week, the photo of a young black bear testing the strength of a hammock on the outskirts of Moab had made front-page news in the local paper. The vise grip of drought has driven the animals from the high country, to scrounge in more unlikely and riskier places. But compared to their Alaskan or Canadian cousins, the bears of this region are still rather shy. If, however, the pressure on resources continues to mount, it is only a matter of time until their interests will collide with our own—with predictable outcomes.

The status of desert bears has been precarious ever since the first wagons arrived here. A tight-fisted environment naturally curbs their numbers. It forces the largest land-borne flesh-eaters and their smaller cousins to be mobile and quite catholic in their appetites. In spite of this, grizzlies haunted the pinyon-juniper expanses of the Southwest as part of their seasonal round until around 1850. Mountain men and explorers contributed to their demise. Members of the Lewis and Clark expedition alone killed more than forty of the tribe of Old Ephraim. (Some as scientific specimens, but mostly for food and grease.) That is more than most modern westerners are likely to encounter in a lifetime. Considered a threat to livestock and man's sense of superiority, ranchers, sheepherders, and government trappers then waged a lengthy war of extermination against the beast of ferocious reputation. It ended in 1979, with the killing of a lone sow in the San Juan Mountains of Colorado. Although unsubstantiated sightings have been reported, that female was probably the last individual of a population of *Ursus arctos* now considered extinct.

Cutting this keystone species out of the great chain of beings has impoverished the Southwest biologically as well as spiritually. In the continental United States, the grizzly's wild and free presence now only graces parts of the northern Rockies— the northwestern corners of Washington, Idaho, Montana, and Wyoming. Ironically, it is also being honored on the flags of the two states that delineate the eastern and western margin of its nineteenth-century hunting grounds: Missouri and California.

Like coyotes compared to wolves, black bears have fared slightly better than their more demanding and conspicuous relatives. They can produce larger litters and require smaller territories. According to experts, they can outcompete grizzlies in densely forested areas. Foraging for tubers, berries and nuts, insects and larvae, and the occasional choice morsel of a bird egg or honeycomb, blacks still roam the La Sal and Abajo Mountains, as well as the Tavaputs Plateau of southeastern Utah. Like shadows and largely unmolested, they also abide in other isolated pockets, on "sky islands," forested ranges pushed high above the Arizona desert. But these sub-populations may suffer from inbreeding, because not many individuals dare to cross belts of saltbush and sand, to enrich adjoining enclaves. The genetically impoverished groups become highly susceptible to changes in their environment. Once their numbers have dropped below a critical level, another charismatic predator is likely to drop out of the race. At this point, population biologists still argue about the minimal numbers required to keep different kinds of mammals from getting sucked into the maelstrom of extinction.

Whenever people discuss the pros and cons of reintroducing grizzlies into parts of their former range, passions are likely to ignite. Ranchers worry about livestock, suburbanites about their children and pets, environmentalists about ecosystem integrity. Wilderness nuts mostly worry about nature no longer "red in tooth and claw." But we do need large predators in our wilderness like we need clean air to breathe. In addition to greasing the gears of intricate ecosystems by keeping a check on deer and rodent populations; by leaving tidbits of their meals for coyotes, magpies, and ravens; by fertilizing and aerating the soil; and by weeding out the old and unfit from the gene pool, these animals still a craving deeply enfolded within human existence.

From personal experience in bear country I can say, that the feeling of not being at the apex of the food chain can be disconcerting and humbling at once. Walking unarmed in the presence of eight-hundred-fifty-pound mounds of rippling muscle that can run down a horse at short distance, and facing fangs powerful enough to puncture car doors, commands our respect. It also forces us to encounter the Other—a non-human creation whose habits we study for the sake of self-protection—on its own terms. As a fringe benefit, senses and instincts that otherwise lie buried underneath the veneers of civilization are exposed. Allowed to run wild, they transform us into the hunting mammals we are: brothers and sisters to Bear. The more we learn, the more we are likely to admire these fellow stalkers, joined to them in bittersweet ties.

Their otherness is just one strand in the snare of mutual attraction, much like the perceived similarities honored in hushed tales of shape-shifting and inter-species marriage. It is an old saw that a skinned bear carcass resembles a naked person. Bears are also the only predators rising up on their hind legs; and the groaning of a mortally wounded one I once heard, echoed the pain of a woman in labor. Some wildlife experts advise people to stand tall in confrontations with bears, but warn against locking eyes. Averting our gaze, we appear non-confrontational. Yet talking and facing them supposedly reveals us as human, not prey. Do we thereby also remind them that we are long lost kin?

Encounters with bears in the wild not only help cast the dramatic narratives through which we define ourselves, but also provide memories that withstand the corrosion of time. I shall never forget a spring morning in the Chisos Mountains of west Texas. I was lured to an oak tree by its swaying, spilled acorns, and a rain of broken branches. A rare triplet of black bear cubs watching mom forage in the canopy became curious and lumbered over to investigate. Like a bolt of furry lightning, the sow shot out of the tree, taking a stand between her offspring and me. Her huffing and jaw chopping were unmistakable warnings. Flushed with adrenaline, I slowly backed off, careful not to turn my back.

Near its confluence with Dark Canyon, Woodenshoe wears the beige costume of aridity. Mormon tea, mock orange, yucca, pinyon, and juniper now mingle with ponderosas. I make my bed on the duff of a tall, solitary pine. I don't bother to pitch a tent, did in fact not even bring one. Leaning against scales of bark, I sip brandy and inhale the butterscotch scent of the tree. Stars wheel through a lattice of pine needles like sparks from a campfire.

Much later, the floodlight of a gibbous moon extinguishes them. Somewhere an owl calls, without being answered. I strain my ears, listening for the soft thudding of padded feet in the night. I listen for branches snapping in the undergrowth—half desiring, half fearing.

# 10

# IN LIMBO

*"All things hidden lead us on and on.*
*The root and end of man are secret things,*
*but in this rocky heart of solitude*
*the fearful, deep, primeval silence brings*
*a kind of answer to our WHITHER? WHENCE?*
*A whisper that can almost tell us WHY."*

—Cid Ricketts Sumner, novelist

B URRO WASH IS ONE OF SEVERAL TRUNCATED CANYONS THAT slice through the little-traveled backcountry of Utah's Capitol Reef National Park. The land appears to have been squeezed by gigantic fists. At its core, the Waterpocket Fold runs roughly north to south for one hundred dusty miles, connecting Lake Powell and the Aquarius Plateau. The fault line resembles bleached vertebrae of a whale carcass washed upon some dismal shore. As a result of the earth crust's violent bucking, geologic strata have risen and tilted sideways. Over millennia, frost and rain sapped cavities, cisterns, and fissures from the sandstone jumble, and even on short excursions, one is likely to see half a dozen layers of sedimentary rock bared simultaneously.

Crossing the raggedness of tumbled blocks, flushed-out gullies, and undercut banks in the Entrada and Carmel Sandstones of the lower wash, I soon reach a stretch where the gradient steepens. The torrential anger of countless floods left its signature in the Kayenta bedrock. It sculpted and polished a sea of choppy, purple waves, standing frozen in time: a perfect snapshot of water long gone.

Gradually, I move back through eons, into Navajo Sandstone. Triassic sand absorbs my steps. A shallow trench wavers between cream-colored, crosshatched domes that glow with a radiance borrowed from clouds. The wash has a scrubbed feel to it. The shapes, lighting, the absence of colors other than white, even the smell of freshly laundered linen, betray the elegance and spare economy of windblown deposits.

Soon the trench becomes pinched in a first constriction. It contracts in a corkscrew slot of less than shoulder width. The rock's flanks are covered with a dark, steely varnish, whose encrustations make it appear older and colder than it is; choke stones and tree trunks are wedged fist-in-glove above my head. They are the calling cards of killer flash floods that scour this canyon irregularly during the thunderbird months of the monsoon season.

Slot canyons are petrified abstractions, minimalist corridors, exercises in sensory deprivation. Where rock offered itself to the impatience of water, the desert's belly has split open. Roasted in a fiery furnace, it reveals the guts of the earth. It is cool inside, and a musty smell fills the timeworn passages. Near their deepest, patches of roseate light fade to twilight, leeching all color from the rocks. Occasionally you need a headlamp, and hesitatingly follow its ghostly white finger poking the dark. In the off-season these can be dank and miserable holes indeed. Unfortunate hikers have been trapped with only their shadows for company. Not too long ago, a fellow jumped down a slotted drop near Escalante, only to find himself caught between a rock and a hard place. He was stuck for eight days, subsisting on nothing but air, a puddle, peanut butter, and leftovers of hope. Upon his rescue, he admitted that he had had plenty of time to think. More recently, a less fortunate hiker got pinned under a boulder in Blue John Canyon. Running out of water, he feared that place would become his tomb. So, he amputated his arm. He finished rappelling. Then he walked out to find help.

Of course, these hollows were sculpted by water. But—except after heavy rains, when rank potholes remain, floating drowned rattlesnakes or even the soggy corpse of a raven—there is frequently not a drop of the substance around. No plants or large animals dare to live here.

In a geological frame of reference, most slots are fledgling canyons. They cleave the Wingate and Navajo, and less frequently limestone formations, which lie only rarely exposed in this region. The searching tendrils of runoff follow joints and hairline cracks in the homogenous rock. Probing, prodding, jostling, prying, and raking, water finds lower levels, but never rests. It enlists quartz grains and pebbles—occasionally even boulders—to do the work of eternity. Entire sections of wall weaken and slough off; rubble is sluiced and sorted in a hurry. Yet all happens too quickly for erosion of the flanks to keep up. In the end, entrenching always outpaces the widening.

When nature created these slots, she was practicing for her masterpiece. Burro Wash and Grand Canyon mark the extremes, but forces and principles operating on them are the same. The difference is only a matter of scale. The generic term "canyon" (from the Spanish *caño* for "tube" or "channel") defines one and all. And yet, they defy easy description; they can only be truly measured with the body serving as yardstick.

❖❖❖

It would help to be a contortionist or acrobat here. I have to shuffle sideways for long stretches, switching the lead leg on occasion, to avoid muscle cramping. Where walls stray from a vertical angle, I am forced to bend like a limbo dancer to follow the sinuous lead of stone. I know I would get stuck in places if I inhaled deeply.

At times, I find myself spread-eagled. One foot and one hand push at each wall, keeping the maw from closing in on me. In a variant of this technique, I chimney over obstacles, with my feet against one wall, my back braced against its twin. I am a choke stone turned flesh, a human wedge. The body possesses a memory of its own, and long forgotten moves flow from arms and legs and shoulders, like young wine from old casks.

But the polished planes are devoid of handholds, and stemming up or around corners becomes quite a challenge. In other sections, knobby concretions grow from the sides. I leave offerings of skin from my elbows and knees on the sandstone, hoping to appease the forces that created this funnel. This is definitely not an exercise for the broad-hipped or claustrophobic, and I am glad I left my pack at the entrance. Gap follows gap, interrupted by light-flooded courtyards. These breaks afford views of petrified sand dunes and opportunities to stretch my knotted limbs.

The ultimate experience is "wet" canyoneering. Dozens of flooded narrows and pothole-dotted slots with ominous names like the Chute and Death Hollow, the Subway or the Black Box furrow the Colorado Plateau. Like the famous black box of science, which yields its secrets only indirectly, these pits are unlit, unknown and unknowable places, changing whoever passes through.

The first letting go is the greatest challenge. As you ease yourself into frigid, tea-colored water, your breath catches high in your chest. In the off-season, a neoprene suit is always a good idea.

There may not be handholds to pull out on until the end of the passage, which sometimes lies around a corner—out of sight, but never out of mind. The slick corridor may be too slim to allow full-fledged breaststrokes. In that case you dog-paddle, assisted by a life jacket or a daypack that contains an inflated garbage bag for floatation. You call out with a voice that rings hollow, trying to stay in touch with your companion. Trying to drown out the lapping of waves against dungeon walls. You roll onto your back and look at the ribbon of sky fluttering beyond reach, reassured that there are such things as birds. And trees. And warmth.

I well remember a September day in a box canyon in the San Rafael Swell. The rainy season was over; the threat of flash floods had passed with the anvil-head clouds. Misled by the benevolent mien of fall, I committed to a long swim through somber narrows. About half an hour into the canyon, sliding down rock chutes, scrambling up boulders, wading chest-deep, or swimming slightly supported by the buoyancy of my daypack, my feet felt numb. I began to shiver violently. I pulled out on a gravel bar that was scantily lit by a wedge of sun, scared by a loss of balance, a certain sluggishness of thought—sure signs for early stages of hypothermia.

Fortunately, an escape route presented itself right there. But leaden muscles and fingers that felt as if they had been severed above the second joint had already compromised my climbing ability. When I finally topped out on the rim, my knuckles were bleeding. My heart raced. I stripped off my wet clothes and started to hike. Falling into a trot once in a while, stark naked except for my pack and boots, I was but a slab of cold, pink flesh in a barren place. Slowly, the flame of life kicked in again, and I welcomed the shimmering skin of my tent like a vision of heaven.

Although Ralph Waldo Emerson probably never saw a slot canyon in his life, he knew nature. "Nature is not a sentimentalist—

does not pamper us," he acknowledged. "We must see that the world is rough and surly, and will not mind drowning a man or a woman."

What is it then, that lures us into these crepuscular depths? The attraction slot canyons exert on the canyoneer is a complex and heady mix. Aesthetic pleasure spreads like warmth, as one watches light splash over varicolored slickrock, drip off scalloped walls, or sweep nautiloid chambers. Colors splinter into halftones as daylight fades. Finally, only the occasional shaft from up high pierces blackness, a lone spotlight on a darkened stage.

While they stimulate our sense of the sublime, these grottos and hallways simultaneously exude some reptilian quality that extends beyond their slithering and sleek cold-bloodedness. Slot canyons recall a chthonic past, activating primitive—and normally dormant—sectors of the mammalian brain. Exhausting your body and mind through climbing simply feels good. So does the trading of blistering sun glare for cool half-light. For some, pushing through slots beyond the point of maximum scenic return becomes a goal in itself. The body bans all thoughts for a while to the backseat. And the ability to overcome obstacles in confined places can give as much satisfaction as chopping a cord of firewood.

Failure has a different flavor down here. Failing in nature is unlike failing in society: you are defeated by forces beyond control. You probably emerge humbled, cut down to human size, yet stronger, and intensely alive. Glad to be breathing. You forget that half-lives ever existed; the story of failure may be more exciting than the story of facile success. It may actually be the only story worth telling. I don't know for sure. What I *do* know is that you are likely to come back for more abuse.

Even the tantrums of flash floods add spice to life in these convoluted defiles. The stakes are indeed high. A baby-blue sky may yawn without guile, before tranquility implodes and the seams of reality rupture. The solid geometry of slots disguises a potential to dissolve into bottomless storm drains. It can push you across the ultimate threshold, exterminating you like a rat in a sewer. Far away and out of sight, rain lashes mesas and naked basins at the head of watersheds, which, root-like, thirstily reach for the liquid. It gathers muscle in rivulets. It tumbles. Rushes. Sweeps up debris. Channels destruction into places of least resistance. The fecund breath of decay precedes the omnivorous beast. Red dirt and turbulence follow. Adrenaline pounds in your ears, masking the feral rumbling. Some try to race it. But for most, preconditioned fight-or-flight responses fail. Within seconds of warning, the flood pounces. It peels back skin, and snaps tendons, crushes every single bone in a body, strips away clothes and pretensions. In a final struggle for purchase or air, the realization may surface that there are worse places to die. *But hardly worse ways.* When the raging abates, sediment and silence mercifully blanket the scene.

Deep down however, I suspect a symbolic layer at the bottom of our fascination. The passage from labyrinthine darkness into the light is an image of the scramble called "life." Scenes of masked Pueblo dancers emerging from sacred underground kivas come to mind.

The primordial separation of night and day.

Our first foray from the cave.

A newborn's transit from womb to world.

Eyes opening wide to a new morning.

Spiritual and physical birth.

The reverse is also true. Our descent mimics Orphic searches, promises the obliteration of all worldly ambitions and self-consciousness. We leave our personal histories with our packs at the entrance. And return is never a guarantee.

In a world stifled by meaningless routines and largely devoid of significant rituals, immersion in nature increasingly fits the bill of transformative experience. Short of pilgrimage, walkabout, or joining a monastery, canyoneering opens one of the few arenas left to encounter the sacred. Poet and naturalist Diane Ackerman reminds us of the function of fasting, disciplined meditation, painful rites of initiation, and other forms of self-flagellation: "The official purpose of these ordeals may be religious, but the physiological goal is to impel the initiate into a higher state of consciousness that kindles visions and insights, in a locale where survival may depend on a combination of ingenuity and nerve."

Even the specific forms of deprivation encountered in slots—hunger, thirst, silence, darkness, cold, and isolation—have equivalents in tribal peoples' visionary quests. The individual suffers a ritual death and separation from her community before experiencing resurrection and reintegration. Anthropologist Victor Turner called this phase of change and growth in the dim recesses between nature and culture "liminal." He considered it crucial in the development of mature and well-adjusted members of any society. These days, for many city dwellers, exhaustive solo wilderness travel seems to represent the liminal experience in a nutshell.

There is a place in the Escalante area, where the canyoneer wagers his life in a mile-long squeeze, without opportunities of escape. Just short of the place where the slot takes its final plunge to the river, unruly floods have drilled straight through the bedrock floor. You can rappel through this hatch, or you can exit the gully here. The intrepid are rewarded with sudden brightness and space at the far side of the skylight. Without prior notice, confinement falls away. Relief momentarily overwhelms vertigo. Apricot light pools under a ceiling formed by the main canyon's hollowed-out cliffs.

Emerging from the domed roof, the human pendulum swings between heaven and earth. Time stretches a little, gives, like the rope. Consciousness hums, taut as the nylon strands holding a life. Your life. Suspended in mid-air, above the unblinking tourmaline eye of a pool, not much seems to matter. For a few seconds, all heaviness has ceased to exist.

Out in the open once more, I am greeted by a parched box elder that has taken a stand as advance guard of troops in the lower wash. One final drafty slot, which I expect to become choked anytime by tipsy walls, surprisingly flares into a slickrock cavern. The floor of this rotunda is smothered with sand so white, it seems precious. Where the roof should be, cloud wisps drift across a tear-shaped patch of cerulean sky, veiling the entrance to some other domain.

Sacrificial games or blood rites must have been performed at locations like these. Silence envelopes me like a down comforter. "The absence of sound has its own sound," muses Brooke Williams in his accounting of lives not lived to the fullest, and my ears are ringing with it. It is the resonance of a heart struck with beauty.

Each one of us guards a place like this deep within ourselves. A cloistered room to which we withdraw occasionally, screening out the white noise of this world, longing for grace notes from another. I feel like a ground squirrel in its den, ears pricked for the melodies of spring. Before I start heading back, I pick up a handful of sand. Its grains run cool through my fingers.

# 11

# WHERE THE RAIN CHILDREN SLEEP

*"The history of my people and the history of*
*this land are one and the same. Nobody can*
*remember us without remembering this land.*
*We are forever connected."*

—Anonymous Taos Pueblo Indian

ROM THE DUSTY WASH I SPOT AN APPARITION ON A SAND-
stone whaleback above. One minute it is there, the next it
has vanished. I thought I had recognized the loosely fitting vel-
veteen blouse, pleated taffeta skirt—of a rich indigo color—and
traditional *chongo* hair bun of a Diné woman elder.

By the time I catch up, she has moved on to the next hump,
and I notice that she has two children with her. As a concession
to the twenty-first century, she carries a collapsible plastic water
container slung over her shoulder. We communicate through
gestures and shouting across the distance. I learn they are looking for their cattle. An utterance from the first rancher who laid
eyes upon the rainbow maze of Bryce Canyon springs to my
mind: "What a hell of a place to lose a cow!" The only one my
hiking partner Morris and I had encountered was dead, bloating
in the wash. My nose had detected it long before my eyes. The

blue-black buzzing of flies and stench of decay had been annoying reminders of how precarious, how expendable life is in these canyons.

Like the fantasy of a heat-addled brain, the threesome disappears over a ridge, swimming in sun glare.

In the grid of dirt roads circling the base of Navajo Mountain, Morris and I had somehow managed to miss the trailhead to Rainbow Bridge, near the remains of the defunct tourist lodge. So, instead of following the well-worn pack trail to Yabut Pass, we dropped into Tsagieto Canyon, one of numerous drainages channeling into Aztec Creek. It would eventually deliver us at our destination. According to my map, Tsagieto joins Aztec Creek, which in turn merges with Cliff Canyon, then with a connector to Redbud and eventually Bridge Canyon. Simple enough —if you can convince yourself that an isometric line on a topographic map actually reflects a "true constant value throughout its extent," as my Webster's assures me. More often than not in Canyon Country, it doesn't.

The verdant touch of spring is evident throughout the canyon. Gnarled cottonwoods have softened with pea-green, semi-translucent foliage unfolding tenderly toward the light. The eternal cycle of youth and maturity also shows in miniature forests of seedlings that sink taproots into the moist sand of the creek's floodplain. After the spring runoff, roots follow the dropping ground water table in an attempt to outlast the dry season.

In a heart-wrenching gesture of patience and parsimoniousness, one old-timer has twisted itself around a fat boulder squatting in the creek. Perched on top, its roots embrace the rock, clinging to it against the possibility of floods. At its base, water splashes over miniature cascades of stacked Kayenta Sandstone, imitating the sound of musical scales played on a distant harp.

The air simmers. I can never resist the beckoning of a waterfall, and dive into a pool of splintered sapphire.

Navajo Mountain, whose dome bulges above us, plays an important role in the sacred geography of the Diné. It is believed to be the head of Earth Woman, a configuration of landmarks stretching from northern Arizona into northwestern New Mexico. Created by the Holy Beings, it faces another—male—figure incorporating mesas, peaks, monoclines, and buttes. In the Diné view of the world, nothing is complete without its opposite. And similar to Australian Aboriginal song lines, this landscape recalls the deeds of mythical ancestors.

A geography based on principles of connectedness not only seems poetic, but also fulfills basic human needs. Discussing human perceptions of order and organization, the evolutionary psychologist Stephen Kellert observes: "By discerning a unifying structure in the natural world, we invest life with meaning and integrity rather than randomness and chaos."

Naatsis'áán, as the mountain is called in Diné, is also the birthplace of Monster Slayer, one of the twin culture heroes of Navajo mythology. And during Colonel Kit Carson's infamous campaign to relocate the tribe to the Bosque Redondo reservation in New Mexico, many families sought sanctuary in the forested nooks of this sacred place. People still leave prayer sticks, corn pollen, and pieces of white shell or turquoise on the mountain. These offerings are part of the Protectionway and Blessingway ceremonies, performed to guard against hunger, evil power, and the loss of livestock.

Farther down-canyon, the sandstone ramparts of Tsagieto lean precariously, without offering ledges, and we have to wade in the creek instead. Unfortunately, we had counted on a dry hike and did not bring wading shoes. Tiptoeing on socked feet, like burglars afraid to wake the owner of the house, but actually more concerned about lacerating a foot or twisting an ankle, we slowly pick our way to Aztec Creek.

We soon reach a section named Forbidding Canyon by Charles Bernheimer in 1921. Bernheimer, a wealthy, German-born businessman and self-described "Cliff dweller from Manhattan," set out to explore a new route to the recently discovered monument by skirting the southern and western slopes of Navajo Mountain. He enlisted the help of veteran guide, trader, and collector of Indian artifacts John Wetherill, who lived in Kayenta. The trader had guided such luminaries as Zane Grey and Theodore Roosevelt to Rainbow Bridge. In 1909 he had first reached the forgotten cliff dwellings of Betatakin, in what is now Navajo National Monument.

In 1910 Wetherill became the first government custodian of the newly established monument at Rainbow Bridge. He knew the area like no other white man. The first Bernheimer expedition of 1921 had to turn around after running into incredibly rough terrain at the head of Forbidding Canyon. The New Yorker and his guide succeeded in a second attempt the following year after another harrowing epic.

We follow the tightening rock throat in the expedition's footsteps and are soon forced to benchwalk above gaping narrows pitted with potholes too deep to wade. At exposed crossings, we find crude steps hacked from the rock—footholds for mules or men. Belay posts that are now rotting were used to lower pack loads.

My water jug has been punctured in the mad scramble for higher ground, and I patch it with adhesive tape from the first-aid kit. Fanged rocks and long stretches of wading have corroded the leather of my old boots. Their soles finally came unglued, flopping like wet bullfrogs with every step. A masterly tie-down job with extra-durable parachute cord makes me proud, but seems to affect the blood circulation in my right foot. My calves and thighs are crosshatched from bushwhacking; a cactus spine is lodged in my little toe. For good measure, the palm of my hand throbs with a cut I suffered climbing over a barbed-wire fence yesterday. Under his sweat-stained baseball cap, Morris looks only slightly better. The state of our bodies makes sympathizing with Bernheimer & Co. easy. And yet, it feels like a small price to pay for the wild splendor that surrounds and sustains us. When we are young, or even middle-aged, we rarely notice the day-to-day erosion of our bodies. Entropy, however, is a universal law. Just as this raw-boned land crumbles imperceptibly, one day to be leveled into nondescript sand flats, so are we being worked on until indistinguishable from clay.

My focus on the pain, as well as our benchwalking and frequent creek crossings, comes to a sudden end when we find ourselves boxed in by steep walls and a drop of more than thirty feet. It can only be descended with the help of a rope, but we did not bring one. Scouting the area for another way down, we chance upon a small alcove holding 1920s vintage coffee and peach cans, manufactured in San Francisco. A black rock slab—polished to the luster of ebony by the creek it was taken from—bears chipped initials: JW. It marks the point where John Wetherill had to turn around on an early exploration of the canyon around 1910.

History has a strange way of repeating itself, and we resign ourselves to stake our tents where tougher minds and bodies have failed. We retire early, to get a good night's rest for the arduous trek back.

After our aborted attempt to reach Rainbow Bridge via Aztec Creek, Morris and I finally picked up the traditional trailhead near the lodge from the twenties, now in ruins. A crumbling corral once held packhorses that carried increasing numbers of tourists to the newly established national monument.

Two days later, we are camped under the canopies of junipers, amid rock domes split into matching cliffs. Tendrils like blood vessels streak their faces crimson; water that leached metal oxides and clay from the walls, painted these dendritic patterns. Tufts of cliff rose line a clear-flowing creek abundantly, setting off the old-silver lace of last year's sunflowers. Red buds—tender but already spine-tipped—rim the pads of prickly pear cacti. The sharp incisors of wood rats, possibly of the white-throated or Mexican kind, have gnawed off yucca leaves diagonally. The mauled plants resemble pineapples on their trunks.

These rodents use clipped yucca daggers and chunks from cactus pads to fortify their nests, and also as a cached source of food. Mostly nocturnal, the secretive foragers are better known as packrats—a reference to their habit of collecting stray bits and pieces. Occasionally they even acquire equipment and the shiny trash of campers, leaving a token object in exchange. These prizes are then woven with plant material into the walls of their habitations. The urine and feces of untold generations of packrats cement food remains and construction materials into dens that become harder than rock. The preserved nests have provided valuable chronicles for climatologists, and paleobotanists. They indicate that the current makeup of this desert is not much older than two thousand years.

I check my gear for completeness, then take some time to sympathize with the little thieves. Like them, we snatch up odd observations, pieces of life's debris. We try to braid them into an organic structure: the story we inhabit. *The only story we know to inhabit.* The sum of packrat monuments that were built over hundreds of years is testimony to rat nature and environment, just as the canon of narratives we assemble from scratch forms the essence of human culture. Or so one hopes.

≈≈≈

The spacious junction of Redbud and Cliff canyons at which we arrive the following day has attracted human attention for a long time. The most recent signs of occupation are hogan-like structures built from the trunks of old-growth cottonwoods, patinated with age. Smooth river boulders reinforce the bases of these dwellings. Predating them by far is a rock art panel on a south-facing wall flanking an alcove. Its multi-colored pictographs have not yet been vandalized, which, given their proximity to the reservoir of Lake Powell and the popularity of Rainbow Bridge close by, comes as a surprise.

In the case of prehistoric rock art, the bottle survived while much of the message was lost. Yet the appeal of human symbols remains powerful long after specific meanings have dissolved. The figure of most interest to me here is a white silhouette of Kokopelli, its paint fading to the hue of the sandstone canvas. Kokopelli, a kachina or elemental spirit, is personified in ceremonial dances of the Pueblo cultures. He is often depicted hunch-backed, or bent beneath a sack full of seeds, playing a flute. The deity frequently sports a large phallus and is associated not only with crops, or the rains of spring, but also with fertility of another kind.

Like Coyote, he is a lascivious creator. According to Hopi tradition, he seduces maidens during the annual dances. Kokopelli is the voice of the red earth itself. He is the pied piper whose tune lures us forever into these canyons. The bass drone of bees and the descending bugle call of the canyon wren pour from his instrument. His sweet melody brings on the quenching rain, his carpe diem! sounds in the steady dripping of springs. His seed stipples cottonwood leaves, and clings to lush pillows of moss and maidenhair fern. Wildflowers tease, armed with his alchemy. He is lecher and lover. He is desire turned flesh.

From this junction, Redbud Canyon cuts across to Bridge Canyon, or at least it does now. Having come to a dead end during their second attempt to reach Rainbow Bridge on a new route in 1922, Bernheimer and his men dynamited a passage through one hundred feet of sandstone, in the reckless fashion of many Gilded Age entrepreneurs or explorers. It took three days to blast a way over Redbud Pass. The use of tough crowbars, which were cut from a California redbud tree to clear the debris, inspired Bernheimer's name for this "shortcut." Inscriptions left by his party still show faintly in several places. Listening closely, I can hear the excited shouting of men, explosions of TNT, and the braying of frightened mules, as echoes ringing through the corridors of time.

Next morning, I wake early, to a soft patter on my tent. Gray light seeps through the seams. There is a puddle at the foot end of my sleeping bag, where I forgot to stretch the fly properly.

The Diné perceive these gentle spring rains as being female, bearing fertility, tickling the crops into sprouting. Their polar opposite and complement are the ferocious male rains of late summer, which are frequently accompanied by thunderstorms and flash floods that strip the land of its cover.

Rainbow Bridge, the destination of today's hike, forms one chapter in the storied geography of the Diné, centering beliefs that still guide day-to-day behavior. Accordingly, Nonnezoshi—the Rainbow of Stone—is composed of two beings, male and female, joined in stretching across the canyon. All the rainbows in the world stem from it. The bridge is thought to provide protection from danger, especially danger on water; people travel to it to be healed of bad dreams. According to a prediction, harm will come to all Diné should it ever fall.

Close by, the male San Juan River mounts the female Colorado. From the union of these two spiritual bodies spring the water children of the cloud and rain people. All moisture originates there and spreads over the reservation. Or used to, before Glen Canyon Reservoir smothered the nuptial bed.

The divine beings in the bridge work in concert with sacred sites on Navajo Mountain, at the confluence of the two rivers, and elsewhere, to establish a power grid across Dinétah, the Navajo Nation. The spiritual maintenance and protection of this network of shrines guarantee the continuation of life in harmony with the universe.

This is the reason why many Diné are more than unhappy about what happened to the site. It was first declared a national monument in 1910, briefly after its "discovery" by Professor Byron Cummings—then dean of the University of Utah—who was guided by John Wetherill and a Paiute scout, Nasja Begay. Quickly, the world's largest natural rock span began to attract growing numbers of sightseers. Oral tradition tells of an earlier discovery: a Diné named Blind Salt Clansmen, who was trying to escape the terror of the Long Walk, stumbled onto the formation while herding horses. However, a bronze plaque in the span's abutment only credits the 1910 party.

Offerings and prayers at the bridge are required as tokens of respect, to please the spirits. At a nearby sacred spring—now also flooded—prayers were intoned, for sheep, horses, cattle, other wealth, or for safe crossing of the San Juan River into the enemy's territory. These sacred communications need to be performed during the day, quietly and in solemn concentration. But they have become nearly impossible. More and more often, idle chatter now drowns out reverential silence. Ignorant visitors frequently violate taboos surrounding the bridge. It is, for instance, considered offensive to walk under the span, since nobody can walk under a real rainbow either. In gross disrespect, Georgie White Clark, the "grand old dame" of Colorado River rafting, even chopped footholds into the bridge's back and placed a piton, to allow clients to ascend it aided by ropes.

After a third attempt to reach the bridge overland finally succeeded in 1909, Wetherill had informed the world about a trail of "almost unbelievable hardship." What Mark Taylor has called "the devaluation of easy access" only accelerated after the filling of the reservoir allowed boatloads of thrill seekers to come from Page for an effortless day-trip. (Visitor numbers increased from 5,670 in 1964 to 235,000 in 1999.)

In 1995, the National Park Service temporarily closed the monument. During four days, graffiti was removed and a cleansing ceremony held. But since this is federal land, it cannot be closed permanently to tourists.

More drastically, the physical survival of the bridge became endangered when waters of the slowly filling reservoir threatened to erode the sandstone abutments and to collapse it. Anthropologist Clyde Kluckhohn's prediction of 1925 that the monument would endure "unmarred by the water, ungrieved by the wind...forever" was in serious question. At the last minute, a lawsuit filed by the Sierra Club and supported by many Diné prevented the reservoir from further encroachment. Court-mandated mirrors on top of the span now reflect beams from a laser installed up-canyon, monitoring even minute shifting of the structure, yet adding to its desecration. Given all this, I would not be surprised in the least, if some Diné elders attributed the persistent drought in the Southwest to disturbing the Rain Children's sleep.

Kokopelli's bag has burst, spilling his precious load throughout lower Bridge Canyon. The cottonwoods are fully leafed out at this elevation, with feathery leaflets of Gambel oaks not far behind. White stars twinkle from serviceberry bushes; plump purple berries will soon replace them. Scarlet gilia or skyrocket flashes through the grass, its brilliant, red-mottled trumpets like fireworks shattering over slender stems.

The crown jewel in this gaudy display is a single California redbud in bloom—the tree so prosaically used by Bernheimer to fashion tools. Clusters of showy magenta sear my eyes with a cold blaze, contrasting vividly with the chocolate-brown warmth of dry seedpods. The flowers are edible and taste like young peas; the roots yield a glorious dye. Diné herbalists roast the pods, eat their seeds, and make incense used in the Mountain Chant ceremony from the leaves. I marvel at this tree, which has put all effort into blooming before unfurling any of its heart-shaped leaves. I wonder, do the blossoms, when ingested, color your skin, or darken the tint of your passions?

Without advance notice, the bottom seems to drop out of Bridge Canyon: we find ourselves traversing alluvial slopes way above the crystalline rushing that delves into Kayenta bedrock terraces. Sky-high Navajo Sandstone cliffs confine our vision, but guide our final approach. They are scarred with undercuts, which muffle our already subdued voices.

One last bend straightens out, and I almost swallow my tongue. Oh my god! *There it is.* The most elegant rock span you will ever lay eyes upon. Any architect's fantasy. A rainbow cast in stone, the curve of a mustang's neck, a dream's trajectory. Even if it were small, it would be remarkable for its purity of line alone. Of course, I have seen pictures, but nothing could have prepared me for this. The muscular span seems massive yet weightless. It glows, as if from within, powered by late afternoon light. I strain to pick up imperceptible vibrations from the arched rock—in vain. The only detectable motion comes from a red-tailed hawk, climbing slowly, measuring the blue void above.

After what feels like too short a time spent in contemplation and awe, we have to get going, in order to return to camp before dark. I hate to leave, but feel blessed that there have been no crowds from the reservoir milling about. We do not take pictures, safe in the knowledge that—like the delicate redbud tree—Rainbow Bridge will burn in our memories, unmarred by life, ungrieved by the knowledge of death.

Forever.

# 12

# THE IMPORTANCE

# OF GETTING LOST

*"Practice is finding yourself where you
already are."*

—Dogen, a thirteenth-
century Zen master

"GET OUT OF YOUR COMFORT ZONE," MY SUPERVISOR AT
work suggested one day. "Do something you've never
done before."

So I decided to get lost.

Not that I have never been at a loss in the wilderness before. But so far, I had never put myself into that position deliberately. Normally, if I do not follow a circumscribed route, I am
at least aware of my whereabouts. I may explore side canyons
and slots, ridges and alcoves, but compass or map always keep
me on track.

Perhaps my supervisor was right. Perhaps true freedom and
the opportunity for personal growth *did* begin where guidebooks
and trails end, especially in a time when white spots have been all
but erased from maps of the Colorado Plateau.

❖❖❖

I guess I could have gone to a place entirely unfamiliar, to conduct my little experiment. But—call it a form of regional chauvinism— I am partial to this redrock desert, and simply loath to venture outside. Besides, I could hardly think of a better place to get lost in than the Maze district of Canyonlands National Park.

I vividly recall the first time I stood at the Maze Overlook, ready to dive into its fun-house passages. I thought I had been dropped on a different planet. Ledges upon ledges of smooth rock lay neatly stacked: white, pink, tan, and streaked with black varnish; layers overlapped like melted wax from multi-colored candles. The predominant mode was horizontal, and yet, there was depth. Lobes of side canyons curled from the main trunks like letters of an archaic script. Rock gyrated around me in sensuous moves. Who needed artificial highs when there were places like this? From the surface of this diaphanous membrane grew protuberances of red Organ Rock Shale with names like Lizard Rock, Chocolate Drops, and the Plug. Some were at the same time protected and weighted into place by square top hats of sandstone. Snow-white boulders had spilled from undercut rims onto bloodied slopes of shale. There were no right angles anywhere, and this ancient citadel sent my mind reeling.

"So," I hear you grumble, "he's trying to get lost in a place he knows?" Well, it is difficult to get *completely* lost in a location with which one is somewhat acquainted. In the Maze, you don't have to try too hard. Although it may not be the middle of nowhere, you can certainly see it from there.

I remember the time I was diligently following my map, try-ing to locate a trail that switchbacks down to the Colorado River. It still took me several hours of stubborn backtracking to find the gap concealing the trailhead. I had been fooled by the repetitive sameness of rock fins and ruddy whalebacks. Generally though, it is easier for me to go astray in our cloned cities than out here.

This time, I would leave map and compass and even my watch behind, and choose an unfamiliar corner of this labyrinth as my experimental maze. This time, I would not tell anybody where I was going. If I did not know where I was, nobody else should either. There was to be no signing of trail registers, no backcountry permit or signal mirror, no safety net whatsoever. Lost to the world, I could begin to find myself.

I drew comfort from the fact that hardly anybody stays lost forever. Unless foul play is involved, or a life is taken by flash flood or river, people (usually bodies, or parts thereof) show up sooner or later. More often, they show up later. After all, archaeologists still unearth skeletons more than eight hundred years old from alcoves and ruins throughout this region.

This line of thinking may seem morbid or glib. Next to losing one's mind, death is perhaps the ultimate form of loss—a separation from identity and relationships. But close ties to the land also constitute an important relationship, and people who depend on it for sustenance and self-definition (like many tribal or agrarian societies) feel the severance of these tender bonds as the worst kind of bereavement. So, what could be more intimate than death dealt by a beloved place?

These thoughts mill about in my brain, as I try to lose my bearings. My voluntary Odyssey has left me stranded in the southern part of the Maze, a peek-a-boo land of standing stone. Pods of striped sandstone fins, several hundred feet high, breach the sandy surface. Over several square miles, they align east to west, and rock crevasses separating them largely dictate the direction of travel. The only agenda I have is to proceed gradually northward, to see what surprises the desert holds for me there. In a terrain that offers so many vantage points, in a climate graced by so many clear days, it is impossible to ignore the cardinal directions, which always keep you centered to a degree.

When I feel like it, I squeeze through slits and gaps. I chimney up joints and cracks, inch by inch. I grunt, pull, push, scrape, and slide back. I curse. One mile through this kind of obstacle course can age you a year. Dryfalls and block-headed cliffs defy me over and over. At times, their defiance feels like a personal insult, and I realize I still have a long way to go, on my search for the bliss of intentionally lost souls. When I have had enough for a while, I scramble up and down the narrow trajectories of fins, exchanging dungeons for aeries.

As always, these high places are worth the price of admission, paid in sweat, and skin from elbows and knees. "On top of the world" is a feeling, an experience, not just a phrase: a maniac's board of jostling, crowded chess pieces extends eastward until evaporated by blue haze; the vacuum of the river's gorge stills this mayhem, but only briefly; acres of fleecy clouds mirror the jumble below.

Concepts like "navigation" and "course setting" seem strangely appropriate for this petrified sea. Currents of land sweep hikers along on crests of slickrock waves, and into dips and troughs. Speakers of Southern Paiute have an expression for this mode of traveling. *Mutoo'kwu* or "disappearing under" aptly describes the image of a hiker ahead of you, as they bob over rolling terrain. That person will disappear from view and pop up unexpectedly, in the numerous high and low places along a route.

If the need arises, you can fix a rough course with the help of star beacons. But the tides of canyon country are temperamental, and a direct line is a fantasy. You better get used to this idea quickly. Boot prints in the sand are your only wake. Unless they are obliterated by rain or wind, you can always retrace them. At least to the place where you were lost before—which by then should have become almost as familiar as home.

Out here, a headland can split the horizon without seeming to come closer for days, showing different faces as you tack back and forth. Sunlit pillars of sandstone are the lighthouses by which you may be able to measure drift.

Due to the prevailing direction of swells, I find it hard to stay my intended course. Whenever possible, I follow sandy washes that shimmer like Caribbean beaches. On these smooth stretches of white, the desire to walk barefoot becomes overwhelming. But I know better. Cactus spines hide in the sand, and the surface will soon be hot enough to fry eggs on.

Early on, I am rewarded for giving up the ease of trails. A smattering of quartz flakes like spilled blood drops alerts me to the presence of humans. When I glance up, five figures with trapezoid bodies enter my field of vision. Like different signatures, the same number of striated handprints accompanies them. The iron-oxide pigment is faded and flakes from the wall of the shallow shelter. Upon closer inspection, a broken arrow point turns up in the debris. After centuries in the ground, its edges are sharp enough to cut flesh. Admittedly, this site is far from extraordinary. The simple fact of coming upon it unprepared, however, makes it more precious than many a three-star attraction, of which one already may have seen pictures in a guidebook.

In trail-less country, opportunity blossoms like a flower. Each moment holds endless possibilities. The landscape engages and opens the mind. It teaches patience. It defies expectations, forcing the hiker to deal with frustration or pain.

What kind of personality would result from growing up in places like these? We may never know again. But traces of an answer can be found. They remain in the calm, brown eyes of a child raised on a mesa top in Arizona. They line a face like the broken country, on whose terms its owner grew up and old. Like ashes, they sift through the speech of an elder.

Trails and roads on the other hand tend to limit choices and lives, making good followers. The groove of a well-traveled path is much more than just metaphor for worn ways of thinking and being. Trail cairns are boundary markers that keep us from stepping outside the routines of safety. When we are at home everywhere, when we do not have a destination, we cannot get lost. It is true that trails deliver us quicker and more efficiently. But whereas a young man worries that, by going slowly, he might miss something, an older man knows that going too fast, he will miss *everything*.

In all this surrounding dryness, my thoughts turn to water. There is no need yet to follow the dainty heart prints of deer hooves that may lead to a seep or pool. Occasionally, my steps intersect the waffled imprints of a Vibram-soled fellow hiker, but in these rainless conditions, they could be several weeks old. At least I feel reassured seeing that they do not match the profile of my own boots.

Vulnerable patches of cryptobiotic soil, which covers most horizontal surfaces in the park, force me to skip from stepping-stone to stepping-stone, or to weave in between islands of knobbed earth, following runnels eroded by runoff.

I reach an area where space unfolds with sudden force inside this heart of troubled stone. Between bulwarks of many hues, featureless blackbrush-and-prickly-pear plains stretch, twice as wide as they appear at first sight. The sun prods with stubborn persistence, fiercer than it should at this time of year. Sweat stings my eyes. Where it drips from the tip of my nose onto sandstone, it evaporates within seconds. A gallon jug of water I carry is almost empty, but I still hoard a full bladder of twelve quarts, stowed in my pack.

This is a land without mercy or shade, stoic, self-centered, unforgiving. And somehow sentient.

After a few days of hide-and-seek and scraping and sliding, I am approaching the Colorado. In its vicinity, canyons run perpendicular to my intentions. I try to avoid getting sucked into their drainages. The going would be easier, but inevitably lead to the river, and my experiment could be terminated prematurely.

I follow rock spines separating these clefts instead, as best I can. The pleated desertscape poses a three-dimensional riddle, which needs to be solved with the body as well as the mind. I trail along benches of sedimentary rock, as I would amble down sidewalks. But they always recede into cliffs without prior notice, or end at a drop. I have to backtrack and climb up or down to the next gallery, hoping it will connect. It never does for long. Amazingly, the mind eventually learns to read this relief—to a degree. Talus fields of boulders slip from canyon lips to canyon bottoms and make excellent stairways, for gaining or losing elevation. But in the smooth solidity of Cedar Mesa Sandstone, they are all too rare.

It comes as no surprise that the snake is such a popular motif in local rock art styles. Its sleek physique and way of propulsion perfectly mimic the canyoneer's meanderings, and beyond that, the sinuous curves of the country itself. (Coincidentally, Barrier Creek snake pictographs are often associated with rivers and springs.)

Some archaeologists have suggested that squiggles scratched into steely desert varnish represent stylized maps of the river corridor and its tortuous tributaries. I cannot believe, however, that anybody who lived in a place like this would need a mnemonic device. These glyphs may just as easily represent spirit journeys, or tangled lives.

Although it would probably take close to a lifetime, I think it is possible to decipher and memorize this convolution of space. And once, its inhabitants did. People are capable of forming mental maps of incredible complexity. A genuine New Yorker can probably do without the colored map posted at every subway entrance.

But I still wonder if our spatial intelligence has not somehow withered, or at least been fragmented. Most of us still hold an image of our immediate neighborhood, and how it connects with other localities of importance: the place we work; the places we shop, eat, or vacation in. Do we ever approach complete coverage though, even within a puny five-mile radius? And what is to become of our children's sense of place, now that they are spending more and more time in the no-man's land of cyberspace?

Another question arises. If we assume, as some environmental psychologists do, that living and moving in particular landscapes shapes our perceptions and thought processes, could the linear, cut-to-the-chase mentality that seems dominant in our culture somehow be linked to the grids of our cities and highways? There is strong evidence that even our largely unquestioned, straightforward notions of progress, time, self, evolution, and problem solving are not universal. And lastly: if, indeed our species evolved in open parkland and savannas, a preference for similar landscapes would be hard-wired in our brains and hearts. What then, is the price we pay as a people living in air-conditioned, artificially lit, crowded places, places largely devoid of green, but bristling with skyscrapers that cut off most of the horizon?

After the rains of a week ago, puddles wink from bald terraces, reflecting sky, clouds, and rock—the essentials. Morning light also catches in potholes near the canyons' bottoms, creating miniature suns that burn at my feet.

As an additional boon to being lost and alone, there is no need to keep up appearances. I fall to my knees and sip the delicious liquid directly from the ground, like an animal at a water-hole, or a thirsty man in a cartoon. Above all, the kissing of puddles is practical. Shallow draughts avoid stirring up algae and sediment, and these depressions are often too shallow to dip a cup into. (With a full backpack, subsequent push-ups make for excellent exercise.)

Above the zillionth slickrock rise, space has that indescribable quality it assumes near vertiginous drops: blue and precarious, and somehow cut off. Sure enough, a few more steps bring me to the precipice. I find myself on a rock nose that protrudes into space more than a thousand feet above the river. I realize that it *is* possible to get completely turned around in this country. I had no idea the jade-colored stream would curtail my progress in this direction. At this point, I am not even certain, if the Colorado joins the Green River up- or down-canyon from where I stand.

Rather than move against the grain—traversing ridges and gorges, only to get worked in the process—even experienced hikers may fall for the fata morgana of easy routes. Step by incremental step, the terrain draws you in, lulls you. The points of the compass rose begin to spin. The similarities between one place and another can confuse even the well-hydrated brain. You were expecting to see that arch on the right canyon rim. Or was it the left? As you huff up the incline, it pops up two drainages over, and to the west. Is it even the same span? The breach you swore would lead out of a slippery stone bowl has mysteriously vanished, and a dead-end overhang has taken its place while you were not looking.

It may or may not be easier to get lost while traveling solo. Potential benefits from conferring about position and routes seem to be canceled out by the distraction human company affords. Who has never missed their exit over animated conversation or an argument with the person who rode shotgun?

Losing your way without witnesses is certainly less embarrassing.

A major source of irritation from disorientation, I think, arises from a shattering of the illusion that we are in control of our fate. Getting off-track in the wilderness scratches our self-image as competent outdoors people. The key to these feelings can be found in our hunting past, when a man failing to return home with his bacon before dark lost face, if not his life. This is the reason guys never ask for directions.

Of course, there is also the gnawing of fear deep in the belly. The only circumstances in which panic should be allowed to rise, however, are (in order of severity): running out of water or food, being trapped in a hole with an upset rattlesnake, deadlines, or a date, back home.

The latest in a series of gadgets designed to keep the chimeras of dislocation and disconnectedness at bay, is the portable Global Positioning System (GPS). No self-respecting acquaintance of mine would be caught carrying a digital gizmo in the backcountry. Let's be honest—we are a conservative lot. Guidebooks giving coordinates for "attractions" that were until now guarded with jealousy, raise the blood pressure of every hard-core desert rat. And I seriously doubt that even this magic wand could get you out of a place like the Maze. The price for crutches in the backcountry cannot be measured in dollars and cents. It is the atrophying of instinct, the death of adventure.

Once you have immersed yourself in a landscape long enough, it begins to reveal its structure. Like variations of a musical theme that forms the heart of a fugue, principles upon which even the most confusing terrain is built can be discerned. Once you discover this leitmotiv, the land begins to sing. On your way from point A to point B, you can either ignore the rules of composition, or use them to your advantage.

Traveling lost, without a fixed route or goal, creates a Zen-state of spontaneity, in which the mind-body decides without thinking. It instantaneously assesses the angle and texture of rock, hand- and footholds, the orientation and exposure of ridges, ground cover and steepness of the terrain ahead of you. It then chooses the best of all possible routes. Just by looking at a climbing pitch, an experienced canyoneer knows whether it can be scaled or not. Not always unfailingly, as it turns out. But this capability, which is the awakening of a true sense of place and self-knowledge, amazes nevertheless.

In a similar way, ignorance of existing place-names can be invigorating. When new, idiosyncratic names are bestowed upon landmarks, beauty and playfulness walk hand in hand. The same original pleasure of putting words and things together also resonates throughout the best of poetry and nature writing. So, take a hike in Hilarity Hollow! Drink from the wells of Goodtime Gulch!

A hydraulic that almost flipped my raft many years ago is not marked on maps, but unfortunately is still known as Michael's Hole. For sheer whimsy though, it is hard to beat some of the official toponyms in this region. Two of my favorites are Blondie Knoll and Batty Pass.

Somewhere along my travels and travails, I find a birthday balloon, cornered by an errant wind. Its paint has almost completely flaked off. But incredibly, the crinkled skin is still inflated, undaunted by the spiny, abrasive personality of the Maze. Longing for some form of companionship, I christen it Wilson, and tie it to the back of my pack.

Like a faithful dog, Wilson accompanies me everywhere I go. But the past few days have been hard on him, and he does not look well. Perhaps it is the shriveling heat. "Don't leave me, buddy!" I plead. "You and I are going to make it out of here alright." Wilson does not seem to hear.

As the sun tilts on its way to the other side of the world and blue shadows creep into canyon bottoms, I rush to find a horizontal spot on which to roll out my sleeping bag for the night. Somehow I manage to get myself into a tight spot on a ledge pinched by a slightly overhung wall. Its outward sloping hand-holds are brittle, and I can feel gravity tugging to pull me backward, off my exposed perch. I have to unbuckle the hip belt of my backpack, letting it drop two stories to the ground. Poor Wilson goes out with a bang, taking the hit that was meant for me.

In good ranger tradition, no body is left behind. Some might say I sacrificed him to save my own skin. But I honestly think he was done for, anyway.

While the peeping sun ignites a rock dome like the golden cupola of a mosque, I take stock of my situation. The pockets of rainwater upon which I depend have shrunk fast, and become harder to find every day. I am down to crushed crackers, some honey, and used teabags. My body is craving fat so badly I could chew plain butter sticks. Worst of all, I keep talking to a dead balloon.

It is time to go home. At first light, I will pick out a procession of pinnacles that overlook the descent from rim to river. And I will start walking toward it.

# 13

# THIEVES OF TIME

*"At its worst, however, the romance of the
Southwest bears the seeds of its own destruction.
It so often finds expression in no more than
shallow curiosity, in a destructive rummaging
through the sites in search of some treasure,
some tangible relic of the past that can adorn a
coffee table, or worse, be discarded after a few
days or weeks as would another plastic novelty."*

—William D. Lipe, archaeologist

I DROP INTO THE SLICKROCK CHUTE OF BULLET CANYON THAT
tilts from the pinyon-and-juniper-blanketed mesa to the bottom of a gullied wonderland—the Grand Gulch of Cedar Mesa.
Rock cairns handrail the route down. It was first scouted for
livestock more than a hundred years ago, by a cowboy-turned-
archaeologist. The name of this branch of the gulch derived
from the common practice of late nineteenth-century excavators to inscribe their names at the dig sites with charcoal or a
soft lead bullet.

I have come to the hot lonesome for the same reasons that
compel more than fifty thousand other hikers every year. Half a

dozen deep gashes in the monotony of the mesa harbor the highest concentration of Ancestral Puebloan archaeological sites. The highest, that is, outside of ancient population centers, like Chaco Canyon in western New Mexico, or Mesa Verde, crouched in the southwestern corner of Colorado. Unlike these major tourist attractions, the rock art panels and ruins of Cedar Mesa are still cloaked in silence and solitude for much of the year. So far, they remain free from the clutter of fences and signs, from garrulous, camera-toting multitudes.

But change is quickly overtaking this vast open-air museum. A permit and reservation system has been put in place by the Bureau of Land Management, which administers these lands. Despite steep user fees, supposedly for the maintenance of this watershed's cultural resources, the number of visitors still tripled within two years. Tourists and locals alike are magnetized by shady groves, sandstone tapestries, and invigorating springs. They are drawn by hard-to-find spectacular petroglyphs, pictographs, and cliff dwellings. Except during the dead of winter or the dog days of summer, one is likely to share the magic with other canyon aficionados.

In its typical stance of trying to please everybody (and ending up not fully satisfying anybody), the revenue-starved agency occasionally referred to as the "Bureau of Livestock Minions" still issues grazing permits on the mesa for peanuts. It costs a local rancher about $1.35 a month to graze a cow and a calf on this public land; it costs you or me $5 to simply hike on it for a day. (And more if we want to pitch a tent overnight.) Largely unhindered, the horned brutes, craving shade, water and lush greenery, trample and foul riparian oases and topple masonry walls that have withstood the teeth of time for more than a thousand years.

At the canyon bottom, an overgrown trail tunnels through dense foliage, like the paths on which mice travel through high grass.

Exotic fragrances hang limply in the greenhouse air, adding to the jungle feeling of this place. The moisture feeds vegetation almost obscene in its voluptuousness. Birds squawk, chirp, and burble behind a screen of box elders and reeds—heard, but unseen. From a stand of stately cottonwoods, a pair of Cooper's hawks swoops down, uttering harsh cries of *kek, kek, kek*. Although the stubby-winged raptors are probably only defending their nest, I feel a little like a character in Hitchcock's *The Birds*.

Eerie bird behavior continues, when shortly after a hummingbird—probably a rufous—attacks a sparrow hawk, reversing their usual roles. The little buzzer's target is almost three times his size. Like a dive-bomber, he circles to charge from above, again and again. I am certain the assailant is not female, since a hen avoids predation by camouflage and freezing motionless on her walnut-sized nest, a nest woven from grass, discarded bird feathers, the tufts of cottonwood seeds, spider silk, and—quite possibly—the light of dawn. In the end, boldness wins the day, and the hummer succeeds in driving away the hawk, much to my delight. The Hopi and Zuni descendants of the people who lived in this canyon believe that Hummingbird intervenes with the gods on behalf of humans, pleading for rain. They use hummingbird feathers in fertility rituals, and embody the bird in carved-and-painted kachina figures as brilliant as the originals.

A handful of named springs are tucked away throughout the gulch. But every single one I am able to locate turns out to be barren. My throat chafes like old parchment, my tongue feels like a foreign object. In a dead-end branch of the canyon, I finally find pockets of rainwater in the bedrock. The treasures these delicate troves hold are still untainted by scum and have kept the coolness of night.

The mouth of another tributary gapes in the canyon's buckskin-colored walls. I climb boulder wreckage, to follow its course to a sheltered overhang where constellations of pictographs spill across the back wall, intricate and intriguing. But my eyes scan the plentitude for just one: the palm-sized, green and brown oval of a human head.

This uncanny painting lent its name to a seep nearby: Green Mask Spring. Only two similar images were ever found, one in Chaco Canyon, the other on one of the Hopi mesas in northern Arizona. In a recent article, the anthropologist Sally Cole argued convincingly that the copper-and-ochre-pigmented image represents the face and hair scalp of a painted, flayed Basketmaker (an early phase of the Ancestral Puebloan culture) head. In a rock shelter near Navajo National Monument, two archaeologists *did* excavate a scalp as part of a female burial. Two small holes in the tonsure suggested that it had been attached to a thong, and was possibly worn around the neck as a trophy.

This discovery further chipped away at romantic notions of a peaceful and noble people living in harmony with each other and nature. Ironically, such idealizations—though widely accepted and seemingly benign—constitute a reverse racism, denying others their full humanity.

A shallow pit close to Green Mask Alcove held the real surprise. One of the most amazing finds in the history of southwestern archaeology: the Princess. The sun had long dropped below the rim on a frosty January day in 1897, when Richard Wetherill, who pioneered the Bullet Canyon Trail, made the discovery of a lifetime. The ghostly halo of his lantern revealed a five-and-a-half-foot-wide wicker basket. After carefully removing a second one underneath, he gasped at the sight of a turkey-feather blanket spangled with plumage reminiscent of the sky just after sunset; a second quilt was dotted with yellow canary feathers. A final basket concealed the perfectly mummified body of a woman, whose body was painted yellow, the face crimson red. With the utmost care, she was wrapped up and crated. The Princess was then carried out by packhorse, and sent to Durango, from where she commenced a long train ride to New York City.

Richard Wetherill was a major player and controversial figure of the budding discipline of archaeology before the turn of the century. The son of a Quaker and rancher in southwestern Colorado and brother of the equally famous trader and guide John Wetherill first stumbled into the limelight in 1888. Chasing stray cattle through the washes and ditches of Mesa Verde, he chanced upon a city of ruins cowering in an alcove below the rim. He christened it Cliff Palace. In the following years, Richard and his four brothers found eighty-three more sites of what they initially believed to be "Aztec" dwellings. Using crude excavation techniques, they quickly accumulated a unique collection of pre-Columbian artifacts that was eventually sold to the Colorado Historical Society.

There is ample evidence to suggest that this assembly of fragments of a priceless past was gained at a cost. The excavators occasionally sawed through the roof of cliff dwellings to get inside. Wood beams are now considered valuable for the dating of sites, as well as for climate change research, but the digging cowboys used them as levers to tear out the back walls of buildings. They also served as firewood, to keep the chill from their bones. (Winter was the only time a busy ranch life allowed for their new passion.)

Three years later, under the guidance of Finnish explorer-archaeologist Baron Nils Nordenskiöld, Wetherill exchanged spade for trowel. Horse-loads of relics were sent to the Field Museum of Natural History in Chicago, and the American Museum of Natural History, as well as the National Museum of the American Indian, both in New York.

When part of the Mesa Verde collection was sold to the National Museum of Finland in Helsinki, a concerned public objected. The Durango sheriff arrested Wetherill's Scandinavian mentor, but had to release him, when he found out that no law existed to prohibit the export of irreplaceable relics. The American Antiquities Act, which guarantees the protection of archaeological treasures on public lands did not become effective until 1906.

Several New York soap millionaires bankrolled further expeditions, including the two Richard Wetherill conducted in the Grand Gulch in 1893–94 and 1897. The desire to hold banded ceramics, dart throwing–boards, turquoise-and-shell pendants, or split-willow figurines never before touched by a white hand, gripped the Wetherills like gold fever. Their ranch near Mesa Verde deteriorated to the point where it had to be sold.

Eventually Richard relocated to Chaco. There he built a trading post near Pueblo Bonito, the multi-tiered beehive hub of proto-Puebloan civilization. Unsupervised by any trained archaeologists, he excavated and shipped a bonanza of artifacts back East, where they were donated to half a dozen museums. The precious freight included more than fifty thousand pieces of turquoise, about ten thousand pieces of pottery, five thousand stone implements, and one thousand bone and wooden objects

When museums began to haggle over artifacts from the Chaco collection the controversy already sullying Wetherill's name only intensified. Notes accompanying the finds were lost, and the collection was finally divided like a pie, sharing the fate of treasures previously retrieved by the cowboy-archaeologist. Greed and collector's mania often went to extremes: a beautifully designed blanket of cottonwood fiber, which had originally shrouded one of the Grand Gulch mummies, was cut in half. One half is now owned by the American Museum of Natural History, the other by the Museum of the American Indian.

The president of New Mexico's Normal University, who was probably also pining for a share of the booty, launched an investigation of Wetherill's excavation practices. In 1902 Wetherill's career ended abruptly, when he was prevented from continuing to dig at Pueblo Bonito. But the final chapter of this charismatic life had yet to be written.

Wetherill has been described as "stubborn, tough and high-handed." He had a talent for alienating the Navajo who lived in the vicinity of Chaco Canyon. In one instance, exploiting their fear of the dead, he placed part of an Anasazi skull on a pile of supplies, to keep potential thieves away.

Perhaps he was unaware or simply disdainful of Navajo beliefs about witchcraft. The ruins or bodies of their ancestral enemies are likely to cause harm to the uninitiated. Most Diné and Hopi consequently avoid them. They are ambiguous sources of power, which can be used to heal, or to destroy. Only witches rummage through ruins and deserted hogans, for mummified parts of bodies that are ground into "corpse powder." Blown into the ears of a sleeping enemy, this substance will kill quickly.

Navajo who worked at the excavations had to undergo healing ceremonies and sweat baths to be cleansed after contact with the dead. The Diné still perform the complex three-day Enemyway ritual to restore harmony in the universe, as well as to protect people from vengeful spirits of the deceased. (Navajo code talkers returning from the Pacific had to undergo the same purifications.)

When the local Navajo started to call Wetherill "Anasazi," he bragged about it to friends, ignorant of the implications of being considered a witch or archenemy of the people. In addition, the trader alienated the Indian agent and Diné who owed him money.

One blistering day in June 1910, Wetherill was out riding the range, accompanied by a hired hand. In an encounter, which has never been cleared up satisfactorily, Wetherill was shot off his horse. His Navajo assailant then walked up to the wounded man sprawled in the dust. "Are you sick, Anasazi?" he asked. Then, at point-blank range, he killed him with a shot to the head.

The enfant terrible of southwestern archaeology was buried near Pueblo Bonito, the site he had been barred from.

Wetherill was not exceptional in his disregard for proper archaeological procedure and cultural etiquette. Earl Morris, the archaeologist who excavated the famous Mummy Cave of Canyon del Muerto in northeastern Arizona in the 1920s, had a macabre sense of humor. Before crating and shipping the leathery bodies that had been conserved in the desert's sterile soil, he propped them up throughout his camp and had a "group picture" taken. His Navajo workers simply watched in disbelief.

Morris also removed some of the more recent burials, ancestors of these very same workmen. Secretly and at night, he shipped them to the American Museum of Natural History, to be displayed with dinosaur bones, rocks, and stuffed birds.

What became of the Princess? She rests in a temperature-controlled drawer at the same museum—in a basement, surrounded by boxes and boxes of artifacts that are gathering dust, but will most likely never be on display.

The era of government-sanctioned body snatching came to a belated end in 1990. After Native American activists had asked fervently and repeatedly for the return of their pillaged dead and paraphernalia, U.S. legislators finally passed the Native American Graves Protection and Repatriation Act (NAGPRA). It protects native burial grounds from smoke-belching bulldozers or ghoulish collectors, and ordered many museums to return bones and mummies and ceremonial objects to native bands. As a somewhat unfortunate side effect, the study of North America's ancient dead, which could yield valuable insights into pre-Columbian diets, diseases, and living conditions, has become virtually taboo.

Before I ventured into this canyon, I had stopped briefly in Blanding, a sleepy little Mormon town bordering Cedar Mesa. Its Edge of the Cedars State Park Museum houses a small but excellent collection of Ancestral Puebloan objects, most of which were excavated in southeastern Utah.

Although usually not a fan of museums, I found myself riveted to one particular exhibit: a ceremonial sash, dated circa 920 A.D. Strands of braided yucca fiber wrapped with more than two thousand scarlet macaw feathers had been attached to the pelt of a tassel-eared squirrel. While the latter is indigenous to the Southwest, the red, yellow, and blue plumes of the macaw had traveled all the way from the lowlands of southern Mexico. They are proof of extensive trade networks that linked this ancient civilization with other domains.

Feathers surviving the ravages of time are as mind-boggling as the irises of mummies that reportedly retained their original color. I tried to imagine the electrifying sensation sparked by coming upon such beauty in its original context.

Staring through a reflection of myself at this garment ensconced in the timeless shell of its display case, I became aware of a sad conundrum. Either these glorious embodiments of past lives were separated from their places of origin—losing much of their meaning—or else strangers' hands would take hold, to hide them forever in private collections.

And this threat is still very real.

Idyllic Blanding has been called "home to the nastiest and most serious pothunters in the West." Fortunes that were lost in slumping cattle operations have been regained and multiplied in the "ruins racket." The latest in a number of cases that have made headlines entails a local rancher. His property includes a site, which could be the largest aboriginal settlement in Utah. It is roughly a mile long and contains no less than ninety-three separate structures. Through a Web site, the landowner sells not only artifacts, but also the opportunity to dig on his land and to keep what you find: for $2,500 a day. Since the Antiquities Act only pertains to public lands, this is perfectly legal. In Utah, even if an excavator chances upon a human-burial site on his own land, he is required only to notify the local sheriff, who is most likely a friend or kin.

Next to cattle at the public trough, private property is the other sacred cow of the West. Although the United States has agreements with foreign countries that prohibit the import or sale of pre-Columbian artifacts, such rarities regularly show up in the auction catalogues of respected houses like Christie's or Sotheby's. Accompanied by faked documentation, they fetch astronomical sums.

Ruin sites in the Grand Gulch have been looted repeatedly, especially during the winter months, when the ranger station at Kane Gulch was vacant. In addition to the loss of valuable artifacts, looting disturbs soils fertile with clues to the past. It messes up stratifications that allow the dating of objects. The analysis of coprolites (human feces preserved in a dry climate), pollen, and seeds in ancient trash heaps reveals details about Anasazi diet and diseases. Household middens even shed light on climatic changes and people's responses to them.

I wonder how well cavalier attitudes toward Indian "curios" would hold up if the sell-out of white history were at stake? Why not put George Washington's or your grandfather's skull on display to a gawking crowd of "Third World" visitors?

Diné weavers shake their heads with incomprehension when rugs, made to sit on, end up as collectors' items and investments on the walls of middle-class homes. But most of us share the pack-rat mentality to a degree. Who has not felt the desire to pocket a finely sculpted arrowhead, multifaceted, and sharp as a razor? Especially since the next hiker to come upon it is likely to do the same. Perhaps it is the quest for beauty in a time when many goods are exceedingly ugly and mass-produced that triggers such asocial behavior.

By stealing from the dead, we deprive the living of knowledge and the joy and excitement of spontaneous discovery. While the Archaeological Resources Protection Act (ARPA) of 1979 is specifically geared toward prosecution and threatens serious penalties, violators still need to be caught with their hands in the dirt, to get sentenced.

The desire to possess and accumulate fragments of the past can at least be understood intellectually. The nihilism that drives acts of vandalism, on the other hand, defies comprehension. In the footsteps of uneducated cowpokes who riddled ancient rock art panels with bullets and used "Moqui" masonry to build fire rings, follow nobodies eager to leave their mark on the world. Instances of defacement are not rare exceptions anymore. Graffiti is ubiquitous in the canyons.

The National Park Service has been forced to put a ranger at the Great Gallery of Horseshoe Canyon, a rock art frieze several hundred feet long that has set the standard for a style known as Barrier Creek. Each day of the busy tourist season, between sunset and sunrise, a friendly bearded giant with a voice that seems too loud for the place gives background information to the curious. His foremost duty, however, is the protection of the silent procession marching across the cliff face.

The BLM had to secure access routes and the interiors of several ruins in the canyons of Cedar Mesa with motion detectors and automatic cameras. (Smile, as you have your picture taken!)

But in spite of promised rewards and perpetrators' signatures left on the rocks, the chances of tracking them down are slim.

Unfortunately, graffiti of the "Kilroy was here" variety scrawled next to rock art is not the worst. My skin still crawls with the memory of "Private Property Keep Out!" spray-painted across an array of Miro-style pictographs, at a shelter in Nine Mile Canyon. An acquaintance surprised a troop of scouts using the beam-and-plaster roof of a kiva as a trampoline while the scout leaders stood by and watched. About a year ago, a number of pictographs in the Moab area that were important enough to bear individual names, were simply rubbed out, including the unique Blue Bison.

One of the worst incidents of vandalism I have ever come across was a badly damaged Basketmaker pictograph in a side canyon of the Paria River. Using a circular saw, somebody had tried to cut the painting en bloc from the cliff, probably to immure it in a natural stone fireplace, next to his Roy Rogers wagon-wheel lamp. Deep grooves framed the image. But the attempt had probably been aborted when vibrations from the power tool caused the brittle sandstone images to flake, or the thief was interrupted.

The list of violated sites could go on forever.

True fans of pre-Columbian rock art and ruins have become very protective of favorite sites, and trade information about them with the secrecy of drug dealers. The National Park Service slogan "take nothing but pictures, leave nothing but footprints" has been taken a step further. It has become customary for the conscientious to wipe away tracks that could lead looters or vandals to an otherwise inconspicuous site.

Many writers also go to great lengths to disguise the locations of intact pots or unusual ruins. But in spite of precautions, locations have been identified—sometimes from accompanying photographs—and objects removed from where they belong. Black sheep tend to anger the Moab community, and the author of a new guidebook to Cedar Mesa that includes GPS coordinates for dozens of little-known rock art sites better not have a book signing in this town.

Even prudent visitors can unknowingly cause lasting damage. Some photographers chalk the outlines of faded pictographs, to make them more visible in their pictures. Plaster casts are occasionally taken of petroglyphs, damaging their fragile relief. The wish to bridge the gaps of time is understandable and probably shared by most sensible human beings. But even placing your palm onto a handprint thousands of years old will ultimately destroy it, through natural oils and sweat that eat away at the pigments.

One cannot help but wonder if precedents of government-financed acts of destruction quietly sanctioned the widespread desecration of our pre-colonial past. In the late 1950s, while David Brower and the Sierra Club failed to rally in protest of the damming of the Colorado River in Glen Canyon, one of the most heroic campaigns in the history of North American archaeology was launched. For eight summers, between 1956 and 1963, teams of archaeologists and volunteers from the universities of Utah and the Museum of Northern Arizona were racing the rising waters. Floating down the doomed canyon, they tried to inventory and document as many of the threatened prehistoric and historic sites as possible. Thousands of ruins, inscriptions, petroglyphs, pictographs, burials, Moqui steps, and assemblages of chipped flint and broken ceramics could not be salvaged. They had to be left in the magnificent canyons that were soon to become crypts. When the Bureau of Reclamation closed the dam's diversion tunnels, the inheritance of *all* Americans disappeared.

Where long ago people leaned against sun-soaked walls, coiling baskets and braiding rope, watching naked children splash in the shallows below, silt now settles on kiva roofs. Fish swim through doorways and windows. Images praising the life-giving power of rain and the fertility of springs dissolve in the depths. Gone is the fluting of canyon wrens, the machine-gun hammering of northern flickers. Gone is the swishing of cattails and willows in a breeze. Silence reigns absolute. Even in the unlikely event of a decommissioning of the dam, the alcoves will have been scoured clean. Pots and ruins have already disintegrated, arrowheads and stone axes have long been buried under sediment, several hundred feet deep. But at least, for now, the bones of people's ancestors lie undisturbed.

The junction of Kane Gulch and Grand Gulch broods under the August sun. Ruins of small houses and grain storages squeeze into the shade of a narrow rock ceiling. Through the hollow eye sockets of one structure I gaze onto the cottonwood grove below. Midday light floods the world outside.

Until about 1250 A.D., the fertile canyon bottom supported a stable population of farmers, who were also warriors, potters, masons, shamans, healers, weavers, midwives, and painters. A few decades later, the two scores of dwellings tucked into crevices of Cedar Mesa Sandstone lay abandoned. People had left, seemingly without much preparation.

A black widow guards the entrance to a dilapidated granary, hanging motionless upside-down in her silk funnel. The red hourglass stands in stark contrast to her coal-black, shiny abdomen. It strikes me as the perfect symbol for the passing of a civilization—*any* civilization. Shriveled corncobs and husks, potsherds, bone splinters, and a broken metate litter the pale dust of the alcove. Silence itself seems to crumble. It reverberates from towering walls; walls that are whittled away grain by grain.

Perhaps, time is the greatest thief of all.

# 14

# A SALT PILGRIMAGE

*"You are the salt of the earth. But what good is salt if it has lost its flavor? Can you make it useful again? It will be thrown out and trampled underfoot as worthless."*

—Matthew 5:13

WHAT DO YOU DO, WHEN LIFE TASTES FLAT, AND THE BLOOD thickens like stew? When the procession of days becomes desecrated, corrupted by the monotony of black and red ciphers on a calendar page? Let go of the familiar. Entrust your life to a trail. Let a touch of the sacred be your elusive prey.

Since the dawning of time, the Hopi Indians of northern Arizona's Third Mesa have set out on quests into the depths of Grand Canyon. Although the gathering of salt near the confluence of the Colorado and Little Colorado Rivers is their most obvious motive, personal transformation lies at the heart of these journeys. For young Hopi men, the first salt pilgrimage was a rite of passage, a test of courage and physical stamina. Upon successful return, they were given a new, ceremonial name and, with much feasting, initiated into the Wúwuchim, a men's society.

The charm of salt, one of the essences of life, has worked its magic across cultures and time. "The lovers of God go into the salt and are made entirely pure," rhapsodizes the Sufi mystic and poet Rumi. Lot's wife froze into a pillar of salt when she turned to cast a last look at the sin cities. Nomadic salt collectors in northern Tibet converse in a secret salt language known only to the men, while their yak caravans descend to the holy salt lake. And the Vedic tradition of India associates the mineral with cattle, the ancestors, earth, and progeny.

While I am excited to breathe canyon air again, I laced up my boots for this trip with certain reluctance, perhaps even dread. For most of my life I have been a pilgrim to the twin shrines of beauty and wildness, and spent the greater part of the past twenty years perambulating the Colorado Plateau.

But my time here has come to an end. A job is waiting for me in Alaska, that other place consistently plucking my heartstrings. This will be a leave-taking, perhaps a farewell forever. One of my very first hikes in the region led me to the bottom of Grand Canyon, and a re-visit now would provide some sense of closure. I have come to give thanks to a landscape that has left more than just traces of red in me. The longing for memories that might have to suffice for a lifetime burns in me like salt pans under the desert's glare.

Anybody who follows paths worn smooth by generations of Hopi pilgrims also retraces the mythical route of Öng Wu-uti, or Salt Woman, and her sons, the Twin War Gods. When residents of Third Mesa offended her during a festive meal, she decided to hide the white gold from her ungrateful hosts, beyond reach of the faint-hearted or disrespectful. Each stop on the trio's way to the salt deposits in the great chasm was transformed into a shrine, at which prayers and offerings are given by those who seek the blessings of salt.

The coveted mineral is called *sieunga*, to distinguish it from *eunga*, or regular salt obtained through trade. More than just for culinary purposes, the valued crystals are used in certain secret ceremonies and during healing rituals. But the clans jealously guard many details surrounding the sacred substance. For similar reasons, Salt Woman is excluded from being impersonated as a kachina dancer, a characteristic of only the most powerful deities.

I almost didn't even make it as far as the trailhead. Bob, an early retiree from Tucson, who had picked me up by the side of the highway, did not mind detouring to the start of the hike. On the featureless plateau, we soon became lost in the tangle of dirt roads connecting the Navajo Nation. As I was about to lose hope, a Diné teacher in a pickup, checking on his aunt's goats, volunteered to be our guide to the brink of the entry canyon.

After the rumble of departing cars has faded behind a rise, silence takes charge again. A first look into the gorge is intimidating. Mercifully, as the sun leaks like a broken yolk into the scrim of clouds, blue mists gather in the deep, veiling gullies and crags.

I wrestle with sleep for a long time, perhaps because the moon suffuses my tent with an eerie green light. But my mind also feeds off the journey's sinister aspects. The salt pilgrimage is fraught with physical as well as spiritual dangers. The souls of the dead return to this canyon. From here they embark to the previous world from which they, like all of us, first ventured forth.

In the morning, under the scrutiny of a beaming yet frigid sky things look a little friendlier. Hoarfrost lies on my tent. A segment of the Little Colorado shows in the depths; its turbidity is a sign that the river is flooding after heavy rainfalls upstream. Hopi seekers would have left in the fall, right after the harvest. But I had to work, and now, barely two weeks into the New

Year, my skin puckers at the thought of having to cross that stream. Pilgrims from the mesa left their adobe homes only after prayer and other ritual preparations, including four days of sexual abstinence. At this point, they would already have been walking for two or three days.

Two tall rock cairns on the edge pinpoint the entry to this turning-and-twisting underworld. Before I hoist my backpack I toss pinches of cornmeal to the four directions, beginning by facing the pale disc of rising sun. If approached with pure heart, Tawa the sun god will grant good weather and safe wayfaring in return.

A treacherous chute of scree immediately absorbs my attention. The heavy pack wants to push me over face first, and my legs are about to buckle. At the first opportunity to look up, breathe, and relax, I behold a grandiose rock pinnacle thrusting up from the slope. This is Polongahoya, the younger of the Warrior Twins. When he became tired on the march he turned to stone. Now he marks and guards the threshold of the sacred realm. Petroglyphs of the sun and various insects nearby emphasize the significance of this first shrine inside the canyon.

I struggle across boulders and break frequently. At some point I pick up a plastic water bottle with a traditional-looking rawhide carrying sling. The trail is surprisingly well defined. It eventually levels off at a broad terrace, more than a thousand feet below the rim. Then it crosses to the west side of Bekihatso Wash, topping the Redwall cliffs—one of the great sights of Grand Canyon and its branches. A maw of gray limestone lurks to my left. Ravenous. Waiting for just one slip of the foot or tongue.

An overhang smudged with a negative handprint and some yellow pictographs might well be the cave of Masau'u, god of fire and death. Prayer feathers and cornmeal were habitually left on a grindstone inside and inspected again when the pilgrims returned. If green corn or pieces of fresh watermelon rind were found in its place, rain would soon come to the mesas, and crops would be plentiful. Something very old, like shriveled corncobs or dried beans, was considered a bad omen, foreboding illness or drought. Farther along on the sloping hips of the canyon, piles of fist-sized limestone and agate top two boulders. I add a rock to these shrines of the Mudhead Kachinas and proceed down the trail. Within view of the river, a breach cleaves unexpectedly in the Redwall formation. After some sliding and scraping through loose gravel, I hit rock bottom in Salt Trail Canyon.

It must be close to noon. By now, the January sun and involved descent have drenched my T-shirt, making it cling to my ribs. It also feels as if I have watered every bush between here and the rim. A sweet spring clucking from between boulders stills the fires of my thirst, while the river's rushing soothes the rest of me with cold caresses. Resting, I snack on a handful of smoked salted almonds.

In contrast to other condiments, salt is truly the spice of life. Warm-blooded organisms need to replace it as they urinate and sweat. Human perspiration contains five times the amount of salt normally found in our blood, and every hiker is familiar with white stains on a bandanna or T-shirt that has been worn too long. One to two grams of salt per day are sufficient to compensate for the loss. Under normal conditions, we ingest enough hidden salts in highly processed and cured foods like sausage, bacon, or cheese to get by. In fact, diets too rich in sodium, which result in high blood pressure, have become a national health problem in overdeveloped countries.

With a typical backpacking menu of noodles, rice, beans, dried fruit, and granola—as well as a Hopi fare largely consisting of beans, squash, and cornmeal—salt has to be supplemented. After many days of strenuous hiking under a brutal sun, long-distance walkers begin to crave salty junk foods: potato chips, peanuts, saltines, even bouillon cubes. Desert bighorn sheep that wearily approach salt licks at dusk are obeying the same call. Among the few possessions medieval pilgrims carried en route to the Holy Land were bread and salt. In desiccating climes, whether in Palestine or the North American deserts, sodium is at least as much a necessity as carbohydrates are.

If salt depletion becomes too severe, muscles cramp; but spasms can also be caused by lack of potassium. The human body is three-quarters water, which is roughly the makeup of our blue home in space. Further echoing our oceanic connections, diluted salt courses through our blood vessels. Plasma-borne sodium acts in combination with electrolytes, transmitting electrical impulses to the nervous system. In addition to firing up our synapses, it helps to maintain the fluid balance of cells. If you are anything like me, you remember osmosis from college, but have to look it up every time you try to explain it. According to my cheat notes "water migrates across a membrane from the solution of lowest concentration of dissolved solids to the solution of highest concentration." Therefore, if more salt is sweated out than replaced, the body tries to equalize differences in "osmotic pressure" by withdrawing water from plasma, sending it into cells. One problem biology textbooks rarely mention is that this can cause brain cells to swell, sudden seizures, and, if untreated, death.

As a last resort, deprived hikers may chew the leaves of saltbush, pickleweed, and other "halophytes" with telltale names. These "salt lovers" flourish in alkaline desert soils that kill less adapted plants. By accumulating salt in their tissues, they reverse the direction of osmosis, siphoning more water from the ground. When concentrations become too high for their own good, they flush excess salt into bladder-like leaf hairs on the surface, which eventually burst. This explains the scabby, gray-greenish look of these shrubs.

The next two miles down the gorge of the Little Colorado resemble the Via Dolorosa, traditionally measured by pilgrims with bare feet, or the length of their prostrated bodies. Here, tamarisk, catclaw acacia, and mesquite choke the river's gullet. Opting for the talus above the recalcitrant greenery proves to be equally painful: brambles ensnare my feet, attempting to trip me; thorns *still* rake my flesh; and limestone boulders with edges like razor clams take an additional toll. My pack is crammed with climbing gear, wading shoes, water, warm clothes, tent, books, maps, a week's supply of food...and my calf and thigh muscles burn with every step.

Just as I am about to collapse, a huge yellowish mound shows above the underbrush like an earthen breast. I have reached the Sípapu, one of the holiest places of the Four Corners region. It rivals even the Hopi salt mines in importance.

The travertine dome houses a spring, whose name relates to a Hopi word for "navel" or "umbilical cord." Through the hole on top, all people first emerged into this world. According to a cosmology thousands of years old, our present world is the last in a series of four. Tawa created First World from his own substance. He then peopled it with mythical characters like Grandmother Spider and the Twin War Gods. In a mirror image of evolution, creatures changed from insect-like to mammalian to human in consecutive worlds. A deluge destroyed Third World, after people had ceased to take care of each other and Tawa's creation. They took to sorcery, adultery, gambling, and other debauchery, and in their arrogance believed they had created themselves. The lenient deity allowed a few faithful to escape into the next world. With the help of Grandmother Spider and a bamboo reed, survivors climbed up and out through the Sípapu. From there, the ancestors of all races dispersed throughout this Fourth World.

Does any of this sound vaguely familiar?

The similarities don't end here. According to an ancient Hopi prophecy our current world will be destroyed by fire. At the end of days, an urn full of ashes will tumble from the sky, consuming land and sea. Some have interpreted this as the foreshadowing of nuclear holocaust.

Relieved to be rid of my pack I walk up the groundswell for a closer look. Mother Earth's birth canal is about four feet in diameter. Inside the crater, bile-green water fizzes and burps. Since this is also where the dead return to a former plane of existence, Grandmother Spider turned the water opaque. That way, voyeurs will not be vexed by strange goings-on beneath the surface.

I lie on my belly and peer over the rim, mindful of the fact that carbon dioxide issuing from the spring replaces oxygen inside the cavern and could suffocate the overly curious. As expected, I don't see the dead. Bundles of soggy prayer feathers catch my eye instead. They also contain finger-sized sticks carved to a point, beads, braided cord, and a flash of turquoise. These *paaho* have been placed close to the water's edge, and not too long ago.

At low water levels the spring seeps from the hump's porous flank, flecking the ground with rust-colored scabs. Not too surprisingly, the drink I take from this outlet with my cupped hands tastes salty. But I swallow a mouthful regardless: a draught from the Sípapu is said to convey eternal life and powers of healing.

Salt laid the foundations for many an empire. Kublai Khan had its white cakes stamped with his imperial seal. Salt has been taxed, serving as currency and commodity. Just as often, it has been the downfall of civilizations dependent upon intensive irrigation. The Mesopotamian floodplains of the Tigris and Euphrates and possibly Chaco Canyon in New Mexico provide good examples.

The agro-industrial Southwest could be next. It is salt, not snow, that often coats low-lying stretches of desert like playas or creek beds. Surface water rich with dissolved minerals leaves an infertile crust after the water molecules have evaporated. These encrustations are indicators of salt deposits that occur frequently in association with sandstone or siltstone compacted below the bottom of ancient seas. Aquifers underlying the sedimentary foundations of the Colorado Plateau can be affected by salt leached from the rock. Where rainfall is scarce, relatively little salt gets washed out of these strata. But where more water is applied to the soil surface—as in areas of intensive irrigation—groundwater can become saltier from the leaching of soluble minerals. Water pumped from tainted wells for irrigation, further compounds the problem. Repetitive flushing and efficient subsurface drainage becomes necessary to prevent the buildup of salt near the root zone of crops.

The same underground salt deposits responsible for the infertility of intensely irrigated soils also account for the tang of many local springs. Below nearby Blue Spring, another percolated mineral—calcium carbonate—lends the Little Colorado an otherworldly turquoise glow. The hue is reminiscent of a glacier's insides, except when the stream is flushing with sediment.

Darkness descends with the sudden softness of owl wings. Snug in my tent, I eavesdrop on the agitated flow. I hope it will subside, allowing an easy crossing tomorrow. My thoughts eventually liquefy, and the stream's ranting carries me away.

After breakfast it is time to do penance.

The boil of the river still comes close to a marker twig I stuck into the sand yesterday. After a good rain it can take days for the water to drop. Under a sky that could not care less, I strip down to my wading shoes. Like a humble supplicant of the deity, or a pilgrim about to submerge in holy waters, I leave the superficial identity of my clothes crumpled in a pile on shore. With a deep breath,

I step into the mad rushing. The water is brisk, shrinking my manhood and resolve simultaneously. I balance gear and food bags on my shoulder. I stagger nipple-deep through iced milk coffee, a stout cottonwood branch serving as third leg. Out in the middle of the channel, the prancing current tries to topple me. I shuffle my feet as old men do, and avoid dizziness by focusing on a point at the far riverbank. My load is so bulky that I have to make the trip twice.

The going becomes much easier on the opposite side. By early afternoon I am approaching a widening of the canyon that announces the intersection with the Big Ditch.

Soon after, I rest on a ledge of Tapeats Sandstone overlooking the confluence. I take in the river's vignettes. A stiff breeze whistles down the main gorge, goose-bumping the Colorado's green skin. The ruddy discharge from its feeder stream mixes only reluctantly with the main current, but eventually succeeds in tinting its entire width.

More than even the town of Moab, this waterway has been my home. I have drunk from it. Pissed into it. (You're supposed to, to keep the beaches from smelling rank.) I have learned to read its quickly shifting moods. I memorized where not to go in a raft. I have slept on it, rocked by waves, the night sky my only blanket. The river has cooled me, rinsed off the desert's dust, and my cares. It has dunked me numerous times. It has chewed me up—though never badly. It has taunted and taught, and at the same time watched over me.

To a young Hopi raised on a mesa yearning for rain, this place must have seemed like the source of all waters. It holds more fluid, more potential for growth or destruction, than he would likely have seen in his lifetime. In a gesture of appreciation, this pilgrim would have taken a drink from the river here, in a time when it was still safe to do so.

Nowadays, pollution from the tailings piles of abandoned uranium mines, from fuel and oil leaking into Glen Canyon Reservoir, and from cattle grazing in the river corridor, makes drinking this water untreated a bit of a gamble.

Artificial fertilizers create additional problems. Too often, the briny runoff from irrigated fields is drained into desert rivers, whose discharge is too meager to dilute it sufficiently. Nitrates from natural sources—like decaying plants—only increase the salinity of streams with high rates of evaporation. By the time the tired and shrunken Colorado seeps into fields south of the border, every single drop left in it has been recycled several times. Fields in Mexico, which lack expensive subsurface drainage systems, lie barren, where salt has sealed off the surface and killed all cultivated plants.

Israelis, who did not build dams as if there were no tomorrow, are forced to be parsimonious in their use of water. They perfected drip irrigation and additional measures to reduce evaporative loss, in attempts to keep soils from dying.

When will water here become as precious as *sieunga*?

During dinner, I have company. A pair of ravens perch on boulders, less than five feet away. Eyes like jet beads follow every move I make. When the wind ruffles their neck feathers, the bases show, soft and gray as ashes from a cold campfire. I have a weak spot for these clown birds, so, against better knowledge, I toss them some crackers. The male swoops in first, wing tips fingering the abyss beyond. He approaches with cocked head, in a sideward hop of distrust. Delicately, he stashes five squares with quick moves, picks them up in his bill, and flies off to gorge himself undisturbed. Both animals appear to be used to people. They probably have a history of raiding ice chests and food boxes of Grand Canyon boaters camped on the beaches below.

❖❖❖

While dawn gilds points of the canyon's crown, renewing its glory, I pack up and start walking the bench top of the Tapeats. At this point the route has merged with the trail of a prospector who lived in a cabin at the mouth of the Little Colorado. My two friends must have loitered all night outside the tent, or else they are early commuters. Now they follow me, faithful as Labrador retrievers. Obsidian wings chip away at the core of unblemished sky. Their swooshing accompanies my steps.

Steep ravines intersect the terraces, and I look for the one that leads down to the salt. It is supposed to end in a drop, about forty precarious feet above a sandy beach. A rappel is necessary to descend from the sandstone balcony to the river, and Hopi expeditions carried ropes of rawhide or yucca fiber. After he created the salt lode at the foot of these cliffs, the elder War Twin, Pookong-hoya, changed himself into a stone knob protruding from the vertiginous lip. In an act of ultimate faith, pilgrims looped the ropes around the war god's chest, entrusting him with their lives.

None of the stark gullies I investigate seems to match the description. Since I am by myself, I hesitate to commit to an uncertain route. My frustration only mounts, when, from a headland, I spot the gleaming of salt far below. Where water seeped from the base of the porous sandstone and evaporated, a glaze of white residue teases like a promised land beyond reach.

I am *so* close. But in the end, I cannot find a way down. Crushed, I return to my pack—only to find that in the meantime my feathered companions hacked a hole into it and pulled out a dirty sock. When they see me approaching, they take off, circling at a safe distance. I am incensed by their "betrayal." They have their own agenda, and it does not include pilgrimage. In a futile gesture I throw rocks at them.

Initially, defeat stings like salt in a deep cut. Perhaps my heart is not pure. Perhaps some are fated to remain pilgrims forever. Middle-aged men *should* know that life is seasoned with sweat and tears. All of a sudden, the lament of a pilgrim long dead seems to ring true: "To go to Rome—great the effort, little the gain. You will not find the King there, unless you bring him with you."

I pull a piece of turquoise from my pocket. I had intended to leave it at the salt, in exchange for a few crystals. They were to be my vial containing the river Jordan, my splinter from the true cross. They were to be relics and talismans, tokens of faith tested, hardships endured, truths revealed. On gray northern days my fingers would touch them like amulets.

When I raise the gemstone against the sky, it blends in almost seamlessly. The storm in my chest calms, the litany of a distant rapid spreads balm on my scratched soul. I look at the canyon. Its shapes and pastel colors swirl in endless variations of one common theme; snow lines the far North Rim like the stuff of dreams. With the transparency and unexpectedness of a bubble, a realization rises to the surface: I already found what I came for. No salt is needed to flavor this moment, to preserve the memory of this place.

I set my slice of heaven on a boulder and shoulder the mangled pack.

# SELECTED BIBLIOGRAPHY

Abbey, Edward. *Desert Solitaire*. Tucson: University of Arizona Press, 1968.

———. *Down the River*. New York: E. P. Dutton, 1982.

Ackerman, Diane. *Deep Play*. New York: Vintage Books, 1999.

Alden, Peter, and Peter Friederici. *National Audubon Society Field Guide to the Southwestern States*. New York: Alfred A. Knopf, 1999.

Armstrong, David M. *Mammals of the Canyon Country: A Handbook of Mammals of Canyonlands National Park and Vicinity*. Boulder: University of Colorado, Center for Interdisciplinary Studies and University Museum, 1982.

Baars, Donald L. *Canyonlands Country: Geology of Canyonlands and Arches National Parks*. Salt Lake City: University of Utah Press, 1993.

———. *Navajo Country: A Geology and Natural History of the Four Corners Region*. Albuquerque: University of New Mexico Press, 1995.

Bahti, Mark. *Spirit in the Stone: A Handbook of Southwest Indian Animal Carvings and Beliefs*. Tucson, AZ: Treasure Chest Books, 1999.

Bailey, L. R. *The Long Walk*. Tucson, AZ: Westernlore Press, 1988.

Belnap, Jayne. "Magnificent Microbes: Biological Soil Crusts in Piñon-Juniper Communities." In *Ancient Piñon-Juniper Woodlands: A Natural History of Mesa Verde Country*, edited by M. Lisa Floyd. Boulder: University Press of Colorado, 2003.

Berneimer, Charles L. *Rainbow Bridge: Circling Navajo Mountain and Explorations in the "Badlands" of Southern Utah and Northern Arizona*. Albuquerque, NM: Center for Anthropological Studies, 1999.

Betancourt, Julio L. "Late Quaternary Plant Zonation and Climate in Southeastern Utah." *The Great Basin Naturalist* 44, no.1 (1984).

Blackburn, Fred M. *Cowboys and Cave Dwellers*. Santa Fe, NM: School of American Research Press, 1997.

Bonsack-Kelley, Klara, and Harris Francis. *Navajo Sacred Places*. Bloomington: University of Indiana Press, 1994.

Bowers, Janice Emily. *Shrubs and Trees of the Southwest Deserts*. Tucson, AZ: Western National Parks Association, 1993.

Breternitz, D. A. "The Eruption of Sunset Crater: Dating and Effects." *Plateau* 40, no.2 (1967).

Brown, David E. *The Grizzly in the Southwest: Documentary of an Extinction*. Norman: University of Oklahoma Press, 1996.

Brown, Gary. *The Great Bear Almanac.* New York: Lyons and Burford, 1993.

Christopherson, Robert W. *Geosystems: An Introduction to Physical Geography.* (chapter: "Eolian Processes and Arid Landscapes.") Upper Saddle River, NJ: Prentice Hall, 2000.

Colton, Harold S. "Sunset Crater: The Effects of a Volcanic Eruption on an Ancient Pueblo People." *The Geographical Review* 22, no. 4 (1932).

————. "The Eruption of Sunset Crater as an Eyewitness Might Have Observed It." *Museum of Northern Arizona Museum Notes* 10, no. 4 (1937).

DeBlieu, Jan. *Wind: How the Flow of Air Has Shaped Life, Myth, and the Land.* New York: Houghton Mifflin, 1998.

Dunmire, William W., and Gail D. Tierney. *Wild Plants and Native People of the Four Corners.* Santa Fe: Museum of New Mexico Press, 1997.

Eiseman, Fred B., Jr. "The Hopi Salt Trail." *Plateau* 32, no. 2 (1959).

Elson, Mark D. and Michael H. Ort, eds. *Archaeology Southwest.* Tucson, AZ: Center for Desert Archaeology 17, no.1 (2003).

Fagan, Damian. *Canyon Country Wildflowers.* Helena, MT: Falcon Publishing, 1998.

Fleischner, Thomas Lowe. *Singing Stone: A Natural History of the Escalante Canyons.* Salt Lake City: University of Utah Press, 1999.

Fradkin, Phillip L. *A River No More: The Colorado River and the West.* New York: Alfred A. Knopf, 1981.

Grant, Campbell. *Canyon de Chelly: Its People and Rock Art.* Tucson: University of Arizona Press, 1995.

Hafen, Lyman. *Mukuntuweap: Landscape and Story in Zion Canyon.* St. George, UT: Tonaquint Press, 1996.

Havlick, David G. *No Place Distant: Roads and Motorized Recreation on America's Public Lands.* Washington, D.C.: Island Press, 2002.

Hevly, Richard H., Roger E. Kelly, Glenn A. Anderson, Stanley J. Olson. "Comparative Effects of Climatic Change, Cultural Impact and Volcanism in the Paleoecology of Flagstaff, Arizona A.D. 900–1300." In *Volcanic Activity and Human Ecology*, edited by Payson D. Sheets and Donald K. Grayson. New York: Academic Press, 1979.

Huxley, Anthony. *Plant and Planet.* New York: Viking Press, 1974.

Jett, Stephen C. *Navajo Place Names and Trails of the Canyon de Chelly System, Arizona.* New York: Peter Lang, 2001.

Johnson, Broderick H., ed. *Navajo Stories of the Long Walk Period.* Tsaile, AZ: Navajo Community College Press, 1973.

Kellert, Stephen, and Edward O. Wilson, eds. *The Biophilia Hypothesis.* Washington, D.C.: Island Press, 1993.

Kellert, Stephen. *Kinship to Mastery: Biophilia in Human Evolution and Development.* Washington, D.C.: Island Press, 1997.

Kluckhohn, Clyde. *Navajo Witchcraft.* Boston: Beacon Press, 1989.

———. *To the Foot of the Rainbow.* Albuquerque: University of New Mexico Press, 1992.

La Van, Martineau. *Southern Paiutes: Legends, Lore, Language and Lineage.* Las Vegas: KC Publications, 1992.

Law, J. P., and A.G. Hornsby. "The Colorado River Salinity Problem." *Water Supply and Management* 6, 1982.

Linford, Laurance, D. *Navajo Places: History, Legend, Landscape.* Salt Lake City: University of Utah Press, 2000.

Lister, Florence C. *Prehistory in Peril: The Worst and Best of Durango Archaeology.* Niwot: University of Colorado Press, 1997.

Lister, Robert H., and Florence C. Lister. *Earl Morris and Southwestern Archaeology.* Albuquerque: University of New Mexico Press, 1968.

Malotki, Ekkehart, with Michael Lomatuway'ma. *Earth Fire: A Hopi Legend of the Sunset Crater Eruption.* Flagstaff, AZ: Northland Press, 1987.

Martin, Russell. *A Story That Stands Like a Dam: Glen Canyon and the Struggle for the Soul of the West.* Salt Lake City: University of Utah Press, 1999.

McNeley, James Kale. *Holy Wind in Navajo Philosophy.* Tucson: University of Arizona Press, 1981.

McNitt, Frank. *Richard Wetherill: Anasazi.* Albuquerque: University of New Mexico Press, 1957.

————. *Navajo Wars: Military Campaigns, Slave Raids, and Reprisals.* Albuquerque: University of New Mexico Press, 1972.

McPherson, Robert S. *Sacred Land, Sacred View: Navajo Perceptions of the Four Corners Region.* Salt Lake City, UT: Brigham Young University, 1992.

————. *Navajo Land, Navajo Culture: The Utah Experience in the Twentieth Century.* Norman: University of Oklahoma Press, 2001.

Moore, P. D. "Life in the Upper Crust." *Nature* no. 393, (1998).

Nequatewa, Edmund. "The Kan-a Kachinas of Sunset Crater." *Museum of Northern Arizona Museum Notes* 5, no. 4 (1932).

Patton, Michael Quinn, and Brandon Q. Tchombiano Patton. "What's in a Name: Heroic Nomenclature in the Grand Canyon." *Plateau Journal,* Winter 2000/2001.

Petersen, David. *Ghost Grizzlies: Does the Great Bear Still Haunt Colorado?* Boulder, CO: Johnson Books, 1995.

Pilles, Peter J., Jr. "Sunset Crater and the Sinagua: A New Interpretation." In *Volcanic Activity and Human Ecology,* edited by Payson D. Sheets and Donald K. Grayson. New York: Academic Press, 1979.

Powell, John Wesley. *The Exploration of the Colorado River and Its Canyons.* New York: Penguin Books, 1987.

Rhoades, J. D. "Soil Salinity—Causes and Controls." In *Techniques for Desert Reclamation,* edited by Andrew Goudie. New York: John Wiley & Sons, 1990.

Rockwell, David. *Giving Voice to Bear: North American Indian Rituals, Myths, and Images of the Bear.* Niwot, CO: Roberts Rinehart, 1991.

Schaafsma, Polly. *The Rock Art of Utah.* Salt Lake City: University of Utah Press, 1994.

Simmons, Leo. *Sun Chief: The Autobiography of a Hopi Indian.* New Haven, CT: Yale University Press, 1942.

Smith, Chris, and Elizabeth Manning. "The Sacred and Profane Collide in the West." *High Country News* 29, no. 10 (1997).

Stegner, Wallace. *Beyond the Hundredth Meridian: John Wesley Powell and the Second Opening of the West.* New York: Penguin Books, 1992.

Straus, Susan. *The Passionate Fact: Storytelling in Natural History and Cultural Interpretation.* Golden, CO: Fulcrum Publishing, 1996.

Titiev, Mischa. "A Hopi Salt Expedition." *American Anthropologist* 29, no. 2 (1937).

Turner, Victor Witt, and Roger D. Abrahams. *The Ritual Process: Structure and Anti-Structure.* Berlin, NY: Walter de Gruyter, 1995.

Tweit, Susan. *Barren, Wild and Worthless: Living in the Chihuahuan Desert.* (chapter: "The Disappeared Ones.") Tucson: University of Arizona Press, 2003.

Van Cott, John W. *Utah Place Names: A Comprehensive Guide To the Origins of Geographic Names.* Salt Lake City: University of Utah Press, 1990.

Westby, Tim. "Off-Roaders Torpedo a Wilderness Alternative." *High Country News* 35, no. 4 (2003).

Williams, David. *A Naturalist's Guide to Canyon Country.* Guilford, CT: Globe Pequot Press, 2000.

Youngquist, Walter. "Shale Oil—The Elusive Energy." *Hubbert Center Newsletter* 4, 1998.